THE WOVEN CHAIR

TRADITIONAL AND MODERN SEAT WEAVING

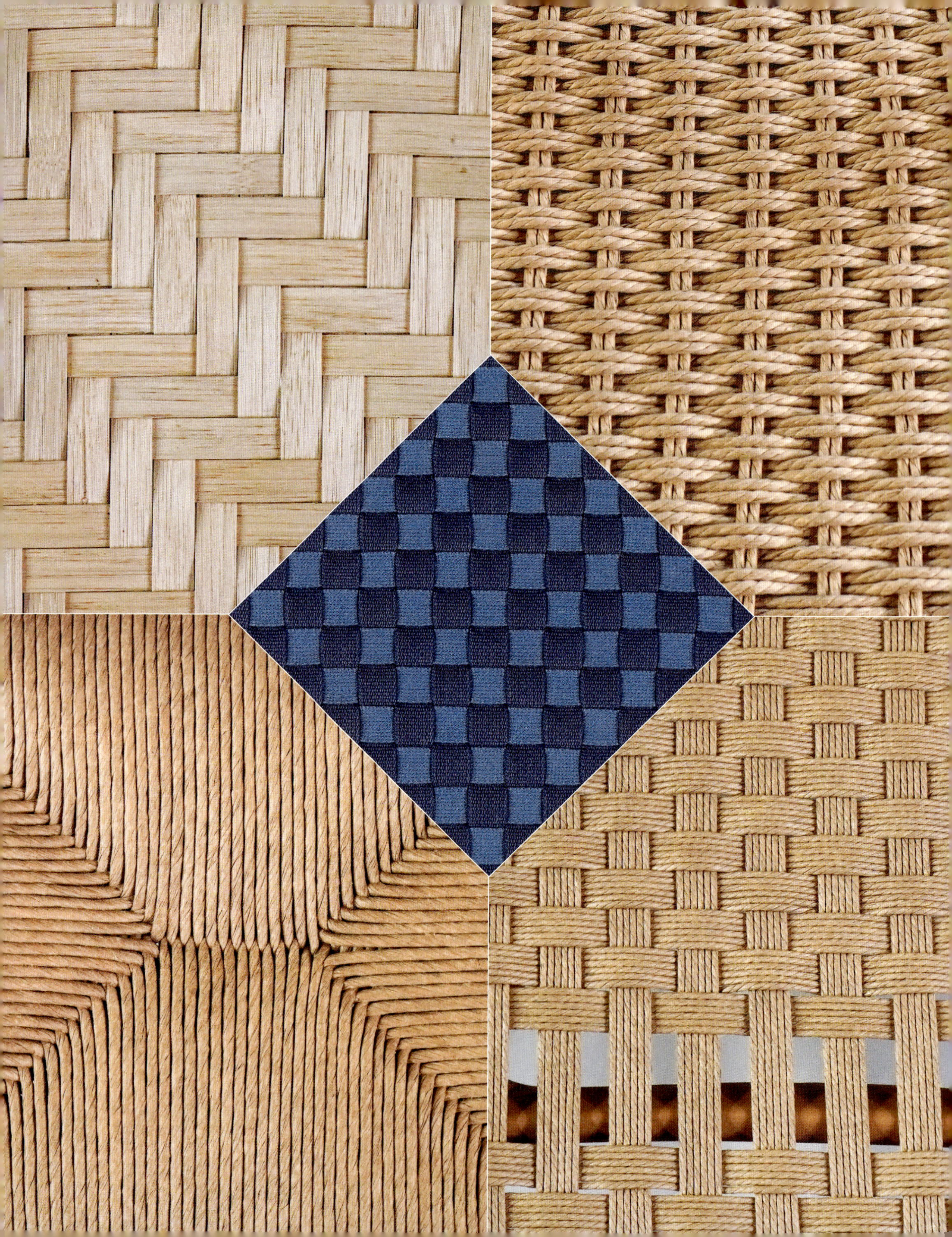

THE WOVEN CHAIR

TRADITIONAL AND MODERN SEAT WEAVING

Written & Photographed by

BRANDY CLEMENTS & DAVID KLINGLER

Publisher & Editor: Matthew Teague

Design: Lindsay Hess

Photography: Brandy Clements & David Klingler

Copy Editor: A. J. Hamler

Index: Jay Kreisler

Blue Hills Press
P.O. Box 239
Whites Creek, TN 37189

ISBN: 978-1-951217-52-5

e-book ISBN: 978-1-951217-53-2

Library of Congress Control Number: 2025942477
Printed in the United States
10 9 8 7 6 5 4 3 2 1

Note: The following list contains names used in *The Woven Chair* that may be registered with the United States Copyright Office: Zinsser, TransTint, Senco, Duofast, Howard, The Real Milk Paint, Titebond, Mohawk, Stickfast

The information in this book is given in good faith; however, no warranty is given, nor are results guaranteed. Use caution when handling tools listed in this book. Your safety is your responsibility. Neither Blue Hills Press nor the authors assume any responsibility for any injuries or accidents.

To learn more about Blue Hills Press books, or to find a retailer near you, email info@bluehillspress.com or visit us at www.bluehillspress.com.

DEDICATION

Thanks to Linda Clements, who made sure the craft made it down the line a couple more generations by putting an ad in the newspaper and letting the chairs pile up until someone caved and taught you. Love you!

To Bob Young who assured us that "It'll get done and it'll be good." Certainly this dedication knocks a few beers off our tab, but we know we owe you many more. Your generosity and support of the arts and human beings have made the world a better place. Thank you!

THE FUNDAMENTALS

CONTENTS

PROJECTS

SHAKER TAPE WEAVING

SPLINT WEAVING

RUSH WEAVING

DANISH CORD

APPENDIX

FOREWOOF

by Rosie, Director of Customer Relations, Silver River Center for Chair Caning

Chair Seat Weaving has been a grand adventure for me. I actually own two chairs—one at home and one at the shop. Nobody sits in them except for me. The humans say they are gross, but I think people like to be covered in dog hair. I grew up around chair weaving and most of the time I find it boring, but I meet really cool people. I admit that it is pretty cool to go to work with Brandy and Dave every day, too. What I do, aside from greeting visitors with enthusiasm and kisses, is try not to get stepped on, make students feel welcome, help catch flies, and let the humans know when it's time to leave and go home. I do this by chasing my tail and sighing loudly. It's especially fun meeting students in our classes and when visitors come in and I get treats. Some students visit me regularly and bring me treats. Some come from Finland, Tasmania, and all over the U.S. I have been to a lot of states and have visited some of these chair nerds, most notably was right as this book was getting started and we visited Sue Muldoon and David Douyard in Connecticut. (David's porch was much more fun than the sailboat or the virtual conference.) I never developed a taste for chair legs, or weaving material, but I do pick it up from time to time to show visitors if a toy isn't readily available. I have to say, it's not a bad life, being a chair shop dog.

FOREWORD

by David Johnson, Sidecar Furniture, Los Angeles, California

"I'm so glad I found you! There's no one who knows how to do this anymore!" I hear this often when new clients bring their cherished but broken chairs to me. What was a common trade is now considered a rare skill. Strange, considering how many chairs have woven elements, but not surprising when these chairs sit with broken seats for sometimes many years. Or, even worse, discarded.

Like many trades, weaving was passed down through the family, a practice not common these days, including in my own family. My kids say my job is boring, and they are not alone in underestimating the diversity and complexity of the craft. With bountiful options on how to use up free time in our modern world, most new weavers come to the craft by a curiosity fed by genuine interest. That's how I found it. While attending The Krenov School (then called the College of the Redwoods Fine Woodworking Program) I saw a fellow student weave a Danish cord seat onto a bench they designed and built. I was immediately fascinated, and after graduating entirely consumed the only book in print at the time on seat weaving. Soon people started bringing their chairs to me and I learned that while many patterns look similar, no two chairs are alike. The differences are vast, so becoming a proficient weaver is a lifetime pursuit. At the time of this writing, I've been weaving for over 25 years and still have many new things to try in this craft. The ability to always learn something new is what keeps my job interesting.

Brandy and Dave have distilled their experience weaving thousands of chairs into this book, so you can have a head start on knowing the ins and outs of the process—typically only available after years of trial and error when self taught. In addition to being professional weavers, they've dedicated themselves as ambassadors of the craft. Silver River Center for Chair Caning is a museum, a school, and the hub of a community of fellow Chair Nerds, a name coined by them accurately describing the community you are about to join. They've gone beyond instructions on how to weave a seat, and explain why they are woven that way. Patterns seem the same from one chair to the next, but upon close inspection they will differ in subtle but important ways. Given the overwhelming variety of chairs it would be impossible to cover all of the variations. But, by explaining the logic of the different patterns and materials, Brandy and Dave are empowering you with the knowledge to weave any chair with confidence.

But beware! Once you go down this path there may be no returning. You'll start to see weaving everywhere. Patterns will catch your eye and mentally you'll be deconstructing them to add to your inventory of weaving knowledge. There're more chair variations than one normal person can master in a lifetime, but they can only be the beginning. This path may lead to basketry, brooms, building in rattan and bamboo, or even Japanese rock tying (look it up, it's really cool).

So is seat weaving a dying art? It may be obscure, and in the recent past was threatened, but if you open your eyes, you'll see it everywhere! Thanks to passionate craft advocates like Brandy and Dave, it's likely that a new generation of weavers will push the craft forward with their unique and varied perspectives. It's an exciting time to be a weaver and a Chair Nerd!

Sidecar Furniture was founded in 2005 by David Johnson who specializes in the conservation of Danish Modern chairs with woven seats. He places a high emphasis on historical accuracy and preservation of patina. He was recently featured in (and on the cover of) Quercus Magazine and has contributed to a variety of woodworking publications. Find him online at www.sidecarfurniture.com or on social media @sidecar_furniture

SILVER RIVER CENTER FOR CHAIR CANING

Silver River Center for Chair Caning is operated by two chair nerds on a mission to cultivate and inspire a reverence for a worldwide chair caning legacy.

Our vision promotes an enthusiasm for the craft through education, published work, community outreach, restoration, innovation, and travel. We value family tradition and an entrepreneurial spirit. We are dedicated to refinement and mastery of techniques and methods and have extremely high standards of restoration.

We aim to dispel the myth that chair caning is a dying art, and want to empower everyone to restore their own chairs. We expanded our chair

caning restoration business into Silver River Center for Chair Caning, the nation's only chair caning school and museum. We teach small classes in person and online from our shop in Asheville, N.C., as well as offsite classes at esteemed craft schools, conferences, and museums. Silver River is an official education center of the Southern Highland Craft Guild. Memberships include The SeatWeavers' Guild, The Furniture Society, The American Craft Council, The River Arts District Association, and we are a heritage member of the Southern Highland Craft Guild (Brandy is a 4th Generation Chair Weaver). We are proud to honor a family tradition, the craft, and all chair nerds (past, present, and future) with Silver River Center for Chair Caning. Our @SilverRiverChairs YouTube Channel has expanded our outreach globally—subscribe for free resources and classes.

The name Silver River is based on a 4,000-year-old Chinese legend about a weaver goddess who wove the stars and light into the Silver River, or Milky Way, as it is known in our culture. Our name is a nod to the global tradition and our first business Planet Art. In one version of the legend, the Weaver Goddess came down to earth and fell in love with a cow herder. When the

Celestial Queen Mother (the Jade Empress) called her back to heaven, she pulled out a silver hair pin and drew a line (the Silver River) between the two lovers. They can only be reunited on the seventh day of the seventh month, called QiXi. All of the magpies on Earth fly up to heaven and create a bridge for the Weaver Goddess to cross. The QiXi festival is celebrated throughout most of Asia, and is sometimes referred to as the Chinese Valentine's Day. Coincidentally, it happens to be the day that a couple of chair nerds got hitched.

When we rebranded and expanded from restorations and informal classes to the nation's only chair caning school and museum, we wanted a name that elevated the craft. An elegant name that paid homage to the ancient culture from which it originated. Most of the chairs that come through our shop have a family history. We hear the unique story of the chair and by re-telling the story and restoring the chair, the chair takes on a life of its own, a legend. We hope that this book will play a part in perpetuating the craft for at least another 4,000 years.

DAILY PROGRESS

Charlottesville, Virginia

Mrs. Clements Caning Chairs for 30 Years

Versatile and artistic in the field of handicrafts, Mrs. Ida Clements of North Garden has been caning chairs for 30 years. She learned the art from her mother who once taught handicrafts in Norfolk. In the picture above, Mrs. Clements is working on a chair bottom. The cane must be kept wet and pegged. With the help of her husband, Hobert, a semi-retired carpenter, Mrs. Clements is now starting to make trays. She also dresses dolls, and during the Charlottesville centennial, made approximately two dozen old fashioned costumes. One, a copy of an 1820 gown made of white satin, was worn by one of the princesses. The Clements have three children, Linda, an x-ray technician at a Lynchburg Hospital; Hobert, a student at Bluefield College; and Donnie, a student at Red Hill Elementary School.

Progress photo by Norris

TOP LEFT
Brandy's Aunt Linda Clements.

BOTTOM LEFT
Brandy's Grandfather Hobert Clements

TOP RIGHT
Brandy's Grandma Ida Clements in Charlottesville Newspaper

INTRODUCTION

Chair seat weaving is a meditative process and the end result is fun and functional: a family heirloom restored, a flea market find rejuvenated, your favorite chair back in use. Not only is chair seat weaving a traditional craft that dates back thousands of years, it is currently trending (again) worldwide in box stores, high fashion shops, restaurants, architecture and design magazines, and with studio furniture makers.

Chair seat weaving is rooted in geometry, botany, physics, world history, economics, and design. The variety of materials and patterns that can be used are innumerable. Though the traditional craft has largely remained the same for millennia, innovations occurred throughout modern history in the typical time periods of the Industrial Revolution and, out of necessity, with the first and second world wars when embargoes on rattan and shipping trade issues were common.

We said we would never write a chair weaving instruction book. There are already good chair weaving books out there. Chair weaving materials and patterns vary widely. Construction elements of the frames themselves create challenges to the weaving process that are too vast to cover in one book. If we were to write a comprehensive book of chair caning and seat weaving it would be thousands of pages and it wouldn't begin to cover every possible exception. Also, there are many ways to weave a chair and achieve the same result.

As we began teaching caning and seat weaving, we found ourselves saying, "The book does it this way but you can do it any number of ways and still achieve the same result." What follows is somewhat condensed instructions for weaving a variety of chair seats ... it's what makes sense to us after weaving thousands of chairs, reviewing and studying books, observing other weavers, and traveling to study chairs in museums around the world.

We attempt to present the theories behind the process because you have to read every single chair to weave it well. This book reflects how we teach in the classroom and we hope it translates to the page. In addition to basic instructions, we've introduced some advanced techniques that may be tedious for the first-time weaver. Some of those techniques will make more sense the more you weave and understand the patterns and materials. It's a ton of information to absorb and that takes time, and more importantly, practice. There is more than one way to weave a chair and we encourage you to try different things and see what works for you. Don't worry, there's not much you can do to destroy a woven chair short of burning it. You will make mistakes. You will scratch the finish. You'll even break stuff! And you'll learn more when you do.

For best results, weave lots of chairs, make lots of mistakes, take classes, watch videos, talk to other weavers, go to museums, etc. Think of it like studying guitar. You can watch a performance and not be able to execute the song perfectly when you try it the first, or the 50th time. You can learn a song perfectly, but that doesn't mean you know how to play all songs. You can eventually play many songs well, but there is always room for improvement ... and you'll still not know all the songs from all the countries. You can learn guitar on your own, but tips and tricks from a teacher enhance the learning process. So it is with chairs.

We learned and are still learning the craft in many ways: Aunt Linda, Andrea Clarke, other chair weavers, books, videos, classes, The SeatWeavers' Guild gatherings, student's suggestions, and mostly by a lot of reverse engineering. Some techniques and tools we immediately adopt and wonder how we ever did it any other way. Others we try out and decide we prefer to weave another way. We get a lot of unsolicited advice from visitors who have been in our shop and discovered the craft approximately five minutes ago. We nod, say thanks, and we honestly do try out their suggestions ... some of them have made it into this book. You always learn more if you are open to it!

Congratulate yourself when you finish every chair ... *before* you critique the work. You can certainly sit on a chair with technical imperfections. Strive for excellence if you are doing this as a business or side hustle. Should you decide this craft is not for you, then you have still learned and accomplished something! You can tell others about your experience with the craft and you can still have pride in restoring your family heirloom.

For over a decade we pushed back against the "lost art" or "dying art" moniker often associated with the craft of chair seat weaving. In September of 2024, while writing this book, two massive rain events flooded the French Broad River, destroying many small towns in Appalachia. Eighty percent of the River Arts District was decimated along with Silver River Center for Chair Caning. The river rose a foot into our 2nd-story location and destroyed three quarters of the nation's only chair weaving school and museum. We were able to save about 100 chairs by stacking them high on worktables the day between the storms. We suddenly learned how quickly traditional craft can be swept away. It felt more important than ever to preserve this traditional craft through our educational efforts and advocacy.

A note from David Johnson of Sidecar Furniture, Los Angeles:

On the night of January 7, 2025, a strong windstorm started and spread wildfires throughout Southern California that grew out of control. Near us, half of the city of Altadena burned to the ground. At the time of this writing an area rich in Black history and populated with outdoors enthusiasts and artists is in ashes with only chimneys standing. At risk of not being able to return are those who share their culture, traditions, and skills with their community. In these times it's important to support those who keep traditions alive. Show appreciation for their efforts by buying their wares and services. Contribute financially or take part in continuing history and the arts by weaving a chair yourself.

By weaving a chair, your hands pass where thousands of others have passed through time and across the globe. You have participated in perpetuating the craft, and as shameless chair nerds, we thank you for purchasing this book and we are proud of your efforts. Here you have it, the book we said we would never write.

Sincerely,
Brandy and Dave

Cane and Wicker are often used as umbrella terms for all styles of woven seating. Technically seat weaving is the correct umbrella term.

Chair Caning is a form of seat weaving where strands of rattan are laced through holes drilled into a frame or pre-woven in a sheet and hammered into a groove. Wicker is the woven structure of furniture, typically with round rattan reed.

Seat Weaving is a vast topic that is impossible to contain within the covers of a book, let alone a single volume. The focus of this book includes interchangeable materials on chairs with 4 rails. We're saving chair caning and related techniques for a future project.

THE FUNDAMENTALS

ANATOMY OF A CHAIR

SPLAT
Vertical panel in the center of a chair back. Can be plain or carved and highly decorative.

CONTINUOUS ARM
Element that provides comfort for the sitter as well as structural support for the chair frame.

SPINDLES
Typically thin, round, vertical elements. They can be plain or highly decorative.

GRIP
Decorative and ergonomic. Comforting tactile element.

POST/LEG
Vertical elements that support the chair from the ground up. The terms "post" and "leg" are often used interchangeably.

TURNED/ORNAMENTAL STRETCHER
Horizontal elements that connect the posts and provide structural stability.

FINIALS
Small ornamental elements at the top of rear posts.

SLATS
Horizontal elements connecting the two rear posts. Can be plain or highly decorative.

RAIL
The top rung/stretcher that is woven around. For teaching purposes, this distinction is helpful.

RUNG/STRETCHER
Horizontal element that connect the posts and provide structural stability.

A difference in rail height is common, but rarely affects the weaving process.

MORTISE & TENON
A mortise is the hole meant to accept the tenon. A tenon is the projecting part at the end of stretchers, slats, etc., that fits into the mortise.

COMMON STRETCHER/RAIL PROFILES

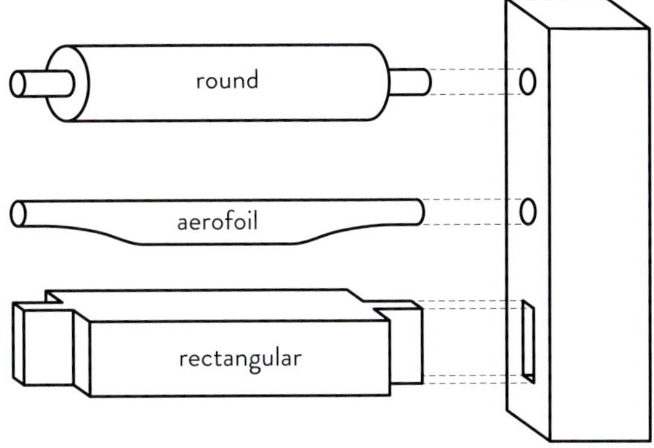

HARD SHOULDER
The tenon joins the stretcher at a sharp 90 degree angle.

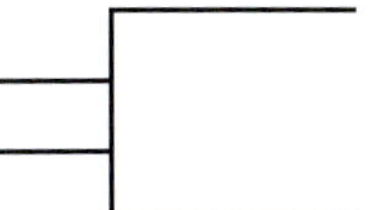

TAPERED SHOULDER
The tenon joins the stretcher with a gradual increase in diameter.

COMMON CHAIR IDENTIFICATION

HITCHCOCK

Easily identifiable by the block corners at the front posts, protective skirts, a large center slat, and honey-dipper turnings on the legs. Most are painted black with ochre stenciling. Also available painted green and we've seen them stained without any embellishment. Hitchcock chairs were widely produced and most with hand-twisted rush seats. The rush-seated design includes square rails with skirts that help protect the weaving. With the trademark and designs changing hands since 1818, there are countless of these chairs out there.

WINDSOR

All structural elements (legs, arms, back) are attached to the seat. An array of spindles connects the seat to the back and also the arms when they are present. Many Windsor chairs are made with a solid wood, saddle-shaped seat, but a woven rush seat is quite common.

MØLLER-DANISH DESIGNS

In 1944, Niels Otto Møller founded his Danish furniture and cabinetry company, J.L. Møllers Møbelfabrik. His innovative chair designs combined wide rails with L-shaped Danish nails that facilitated a single-panel, Danish cord seat. The Møller company includes multiple generations of chair designs, is family-run and continues to practice "production without assembly lines."

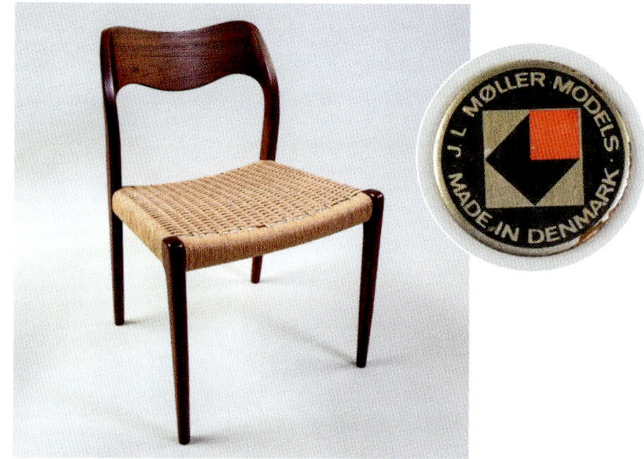

HANS WEGNER-DANISH DESIGNS

Hans Wegner was a Danish designer obsessed with building the perfect chair. He designed over 500 in his lifetime. Inspired by centuries of chair designs, including Asian and Shaker forms, he was never truly satisfied and pursued chair excellence for his entire life. His timeless designs are numbered chronologically and the letters represent the manufacturer. This example, The Wishbone Chair/CH24 was manufactured by Carl Hansen & Søn, while the J16 Rocker was built by Johannes Hansen.

LADDERBACK/SLAT-BACK

A post-and-rung chair with a series of slats as the back support that resemble a ladder. The slats can be plain or quite ornate. The ladderback chair is known for being rustic and functional, but continues to be reimagined in modern designs.

SHAKER

The Shaker community prized simplicity and functionality. Graceful, lightweight post-and-rung chairs were intended to hang on the wall when not in use. Different Shaker communities can be identified by the stylized finials or shawl rails. Maker's marks can be found on authentic Shaker chairs.

MULE EAR/THUMB-BACK

A post-and-rung chair with a short slat-back. The back posts resemble mule ears to Southerners and a bent-back thumb to those in the North. Currently there is a movement to rename these "Poyner chairs" after Richard Poyner to honor his contribution to chairmaking.

KENNEDY ROCKER

President Kennedy's physical therapist prescribed a rocking chair to relieve his back pain. Since then the Carolina rocker with binder cane back and seat has been known as the Kennedy Rocker.

Photo courtesy of Troutman Chairs

MATERIALS, TOOLS & SKILLS LIBRARY

The following section is intended as a more in-depth reference for subsequent projects. Not all of the materials/tools/skills are needed for every project. The reference list isn't comprehensive and you should refer to the intended project for a complete list of the necessary materials/tools/skills.

MATERIALS

GALVANIZED STEEL WIRE

Splint Reed; Binder Cane

For splicing warp strands, we use a wire wrap with 23 gauge galvanized wire. It's small enough to bend by hand, rustproof, and easily removable if visible once the seat is complete. We prefer the wire wrap to stapling, tying string or tying the material to itself. These other methods put more stress on the material and cause breakage.

TACKS

Shaker Tape; Paper Rush; Danish Rush; Pre-twisted Natural Rush; Twisted Seagrass; Yugoslavian Folding Chair

A #3 blued steel cut tack is good for most projects. The ⅜" length is long enough to solidly hold material while causing minimal damage to the rails. Other steel tacks work, but avoid aluminum or brass tacks.

PROTECTIVE COATING

Splint Reed; Paper Rush; Pre-twisted Natural Rush; Twisted Seagrass

We use a premixed, clear shellac from Zinsser. Shellac is a natural, non-petroleum-based product with low fumes. We prefer the clear shellac over the amber shellac, which tends to look orange. When we need to add color to the shellac, we use TransTint Dyes. Feel free to use your favorite polyurethane, linseed oil, or other types of sealants.

FOAM

Shaker Tape; Splint Reed

Putting foam between layers of weaving relieves pressure on common breakpoints (ex: front/side rails). The foam thickness needs to be approximately the thickness of the seat's rails. 1" open-cell upholstery foam works for most projects. If you want to be a little more traditional, use cotton batting in a fabric pillowcase. If your chair will be exposed to moisture, do not use foam or stuffing of any kind!

TOOLS

RAMP

Shaker Tape; Splint Reed; Binder Cane

Potential ramp tools are everywhere! From a simple spoon handle or butter knife to hand-customized tools and amazing forged ramps (that we lost in the shop somewhere). Grab what's at hand or find a favorite and hang onto it. When the pattern gets tight, you'll want to lean on a flathead screwdriver.

SPRING CLAMP

Shaker Tape; Splint Reed; Binder Cane; Paper Rush; Danish Rush; Pre-twisted Natural Rush; Twisted Seagrass; Møller; Yugoslavian Folding Chair

Trust your clamp; it's your best weaving friend! Clamps act as an additional hand when you need them. They are necessary to hold material tension, especially when wrapping the warp. We use both 4" and 6" spring clamps depending on the rail width ... and our mood. The ideal clamp does not have swivel-jaws, is easy to open, and holds the material firmly. A tight clamp will wear out your hands and dent the material.

FLATHEAD SCREWDRIVER

Shaker Tape; Splint Reed; Binder Cane; Paper Rush; Danish Rush; Pre-twisted Natural Rush; Twisted Seagrass; Møller; Yugoslavian Folding Chair

We prefer to use a square-shafted screwdriver for compression. In addition to using the flathead as a paddle, you can use the side of the screwdriver to "pull" the material up/down the rail.

PRO TIP: *Pneumatic Stapler*

Shaker Tape; Paper Rush; Danish Rush; Pre-twisted Natural Rush; Twisted Seagrass; Yugoslavian Folding Chair

To save time and effort use a pneumatic stapler instead of tacks. A small compressor/stapler combo is an investment that pays for itself quickly. We use an upholstery stapler (Duo Fast Model 3424) that shoots 23 gauge, 3/16" crown staples in varying leg lengths. A 3/8" leg is ideal for most projects. Wider staples don't hold the material securely and thicker (18-20 gauge) staples cause rail damage. Our smaller stapler does not have a nose safety arm, which allows much more flexibility when positioning the staple.

In most cases, one staple will secure the material. Don't press the stapler hard into the material. Instead, hover over or lightly touch the material or you risk punching through it. This is especially true for binder cane. You can always secure a not-quite-set staple with a quick hammer blow. If the staple doesn't want to hold, wrap the end of the material in masking tape and staple through the wrap.

HAMMER

Paper Rush; Pre-twisted Natural Rush; Twisted Seagrass; Shaker Tape; Splint Reed; Binder Cane; Møller

We prefer a 6 oz. ball peen hammer. You wouldn't think a couple ounces would matter, but a larger hammer gets heavy quickly and space is tight. Claw-ended hammers are more likely to accidentally cause frame damage.

Don't choke up on a hammer. You'll have better control by holding the handle at the end.

PRO TIP: *Trimmers*

Splint Reed; Binder Cane; Pre-twisted Natural Rush; Twisted Seagrass

Don't overthink it. If it won't cut your face, it won't damage the material. We primarily use a Wahl Rechargeable 1" trimmer. Bigger trimmers aren't as surgical as the smaller varieties and won't finish the job any quicker.

MATERIALS, TOOLS & SKILLS LIBRARY (CONTINUED)

SKILLS

SIZING FOAM

Shaker Tape; Splint Reed

For cutting, a good set of scissors works better than a blade. The foam is hidden within the panel, so don't worry about making the edges perfect. To reduce the risk of seeing foam along the rails or in the corners at the posts, cut it ~½" smaller than the opening and then cut 1" off each corner. If the chair is armless, your life is easy and you don't have to measure and transfer the size of the opening to your foam panel. Simply place the foam on the edge of the table and turn the chair upside down on top of it. Make a line ½" from the front and side rails (the back of the chair provides a natural ½" allowance). Voila!

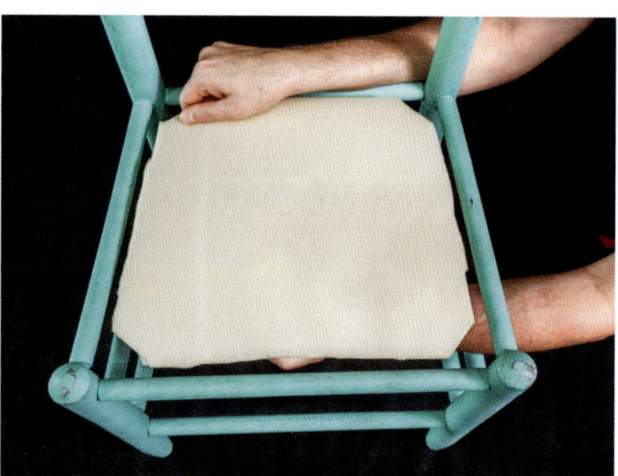

Exiting pattern with ramp.

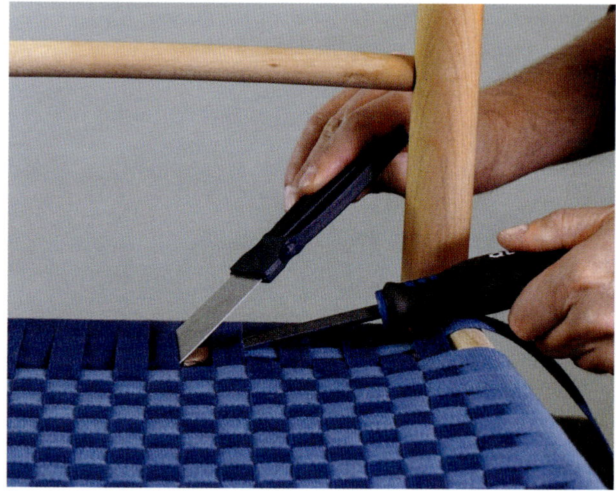

Entering pattern with ramp.

USING A RAMP:

Shaker Tape; Splint Reed; Binder Cane

When you first start a project, it's easy to push weaver strands through the warps using your hands. A ramp tool is absolutely necessary as weaving progresses and warp strands tighten. Place the ramp at a steep angle where you want the weaver to exit the pattern. Push the weaver through the pattern and it will follow the ramp to exactly where you wanted it to go. As the pattern tightens, you can use the ramp to guide the weaver into the pattern as well.

INCHWORM TECHNIQUE

Shaker Tape; Splint Reed; Binder Cane; Møller; Yugoslavian Folding Chair

This technique gives you more leverage and makes it easier to maneuver the weaver strand through the pattern. This is a necessity for warp/weft style weaving, especially toward the end when the pattern tightens up.

1. Make a 6"-8" loop and weave the end partially through the pattern. This is your "working loop" or "working end."
2. Pull the loop taut with one hand, keeping the other hand at the loop to prevent it from breaking the strand or twisting.
3. Repeat these two steps while intermittently pulling the entire strand through the pattern.

CLAMPING:

Shaker Tape; Splint Reed; Binder Cane; Paper Rush; Danish Rush; Pre-twisted Natural Rush; Twisted Seagrass; Møller; Yugoslavian Folding Chair

Clamp "on" the rail and not "over" the rail. Clamping over the rail adds slack into the pattern.

MATERIALS, TOOLS & SKILLS LIBRARY (CONTINUED)

MARKING GUSSETS

Paper Rush; Danish Rush; Pre-twisted Natural Rush; Twisted Seagrass

Most chairs are trapezoidal and weaving patterns are rectangular. The gussets are the triangular areas that result from a difference in length between the front rail and the back rail.

Don't make the mistake of using a square between the front and back rail to mark the gussets. Chairs are rarely square and measurements work every time.

Measure and record distance between front posts and distance between back posts to the nearest ⅛" (0.125"). Then calculate the gusset length.

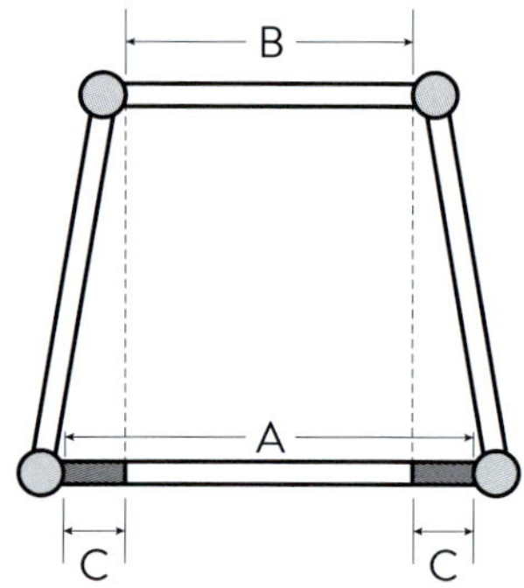

A: Distance between front posts

B: Distance between back posts

C: Gusset Length

$$\frac{A - B}{2} = C$$

Example: A=17.5"; B=15.75"

$$\frac{17.5'' - 15.75''}{2} = 0.875'' \ (7/8'')$$

Measure the gusset length from the post and make a pencil mark. Do the same for both sides. Measure between the two marks and compare with distance between back posts (B). They should be the same. If they are different, double-check your measurements and calculations.

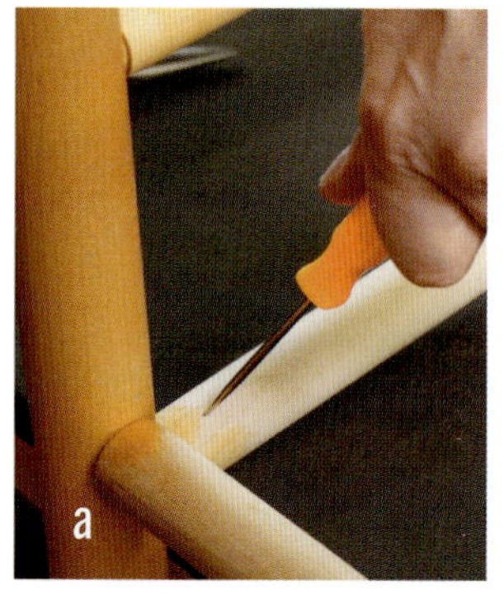

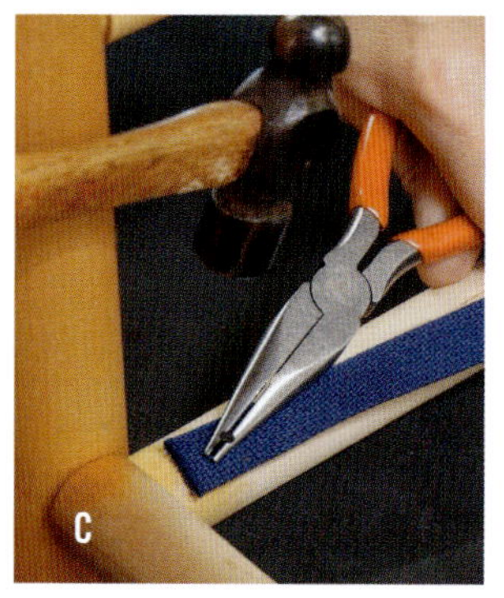

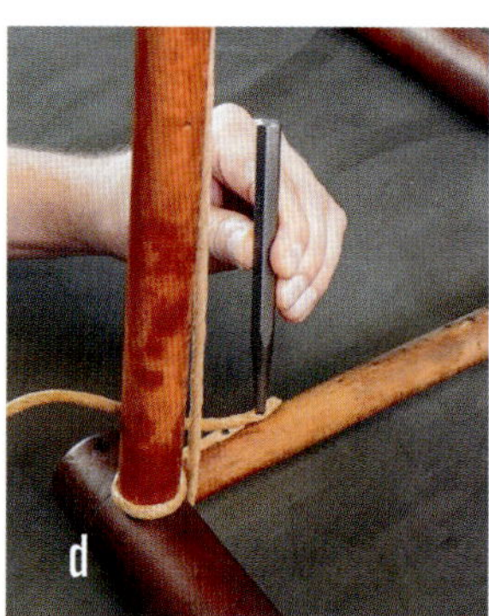

TACKING

Shaker Tape; Paper Rush; Danish Rush; Pre-twisted Natural Rush; Twisted Seagrass; Yugoslavian Folding Chair

A seemingly simple task can sometimes be the most frustrating part of a project. Be patient if you are a beginner. Wrap the end in masking tape if the tack is splitting the material.

- Use an awl to make a pilot hole in the rail. Occasionally, we've used a drill to make pilot holes in extremely dense rails. **[a]**
- Hammer the tack into the material first and use the material as a "handle" for the tack. We use the conveniently located front rail or side rail for this purpose.
- Use needle-nose pliers to hold the tack. **[b, c]**
- Use a nail set once the tack is steady. **[d]**
- Turn the chair on its side. This allows you to swing the hammer down instead of sideways, and provides solid support for the chair frame.

COMPRESSING ON THE RAILS

Shaker Tape; Splint Reed; Binder Cane; Paper Rush; Danish Rush; Pre-twisted Natural Rush; Twisted Seagrass; Møller; Yugoslavian Folding Chair

The goal is to work the maximum amount of material onto the rails. More material lends itself to pattern uniformity, less material shifting and, ultimately, more wear time before a necessary replacement.

Flat Material: Shaker Tape, Splint Reed, Binder Cane

- The strands may look like they're touching, but it's surprising how much cumulative space is available when you compress them together. Avoid overlapping the material.
- Put the tip of a flathead screwdriver or putty knife between two strands. Make sure the tool is in contact with the rail to prevent chipping or scraping across the material. Tap the material sideways along the rail, working 1-2 strands at a time. **[a]**
- When compressing, you can get to a point where there is space on the rail, but not enough space for another strand. Then it's time to decompress and distribute the material evenly along the rail.

Corded Material: Paper Rush, Danish Cord, Pre-twisted Natural Rush, Twisted Seagrass

- Use a flathead screwdriver like a paddle and hit it with a hammer, compressing the material and making more space on the rail. Brace the chair frame with your arm, hip, etc. **[b, c]**
- Rail wraps require compressing on the inside and the outside of the rail.
- Hold the screwdriver above and below the rail, using it to push/pull the material as necessary. **[d]**
- Don't over-compress to the point where the strands pop up off of the rail.

a

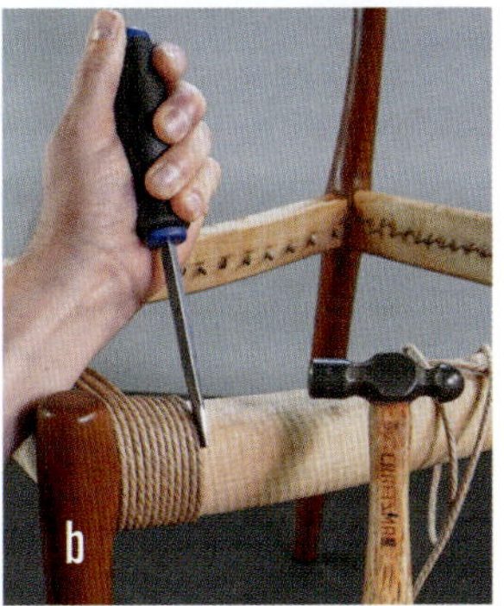
b

c

d

MATERIALS, TOOLS & SKILLS LIBRARY (CONTINUED)

APPLYING PROTECTIVE COAT—SHELLAC

Splint Reed; Paper Rush; Pre-twisted Natural Rush; Twisted Seagrass

- Make sure the material is fully dry before applying a seal. Waiting 24 hours is a good rule of thumb. If we're in a pinch, we use a fan to speed the drying process
- We use a 2"-3" chip brush to apply shellac. Any method you are comfortable with is the best method to use.
- Watch for drips. If you get shellac on any of the wood surfaces, wipe it off quickly with a rag. Brush splatter can be almost invisible, so wipe off the posts and rails as you work. Don't worry about taping off the chair frame. Thin finishes often run under the tape and make a mess that undermines your taping efforts. Been there ... it's annoying.
- Start on the underside/less-visible side of the panel. When you move to the more-visible side, you can clean up drips much easier. **[a]**
- Try not to step away during application or you might see lines/stripes where the new coat overlapped the dry.
- When applying shellac close to the posts, hold the brush close and the thin finish will often flow over toward the post without needing full brush strokes. This is especially true for paper rush which literally sucks in the shellac. **[b]**
- One coat on top and bottom is enough. Multiple coats of finish give the material a plastic feel. Additional coats can be added years down the road if the first coat starts to wear away. **[c]**
- Shellac dries to the touch quickly, but it's best to wait 24 hours for it to dry completely.

a

b

c

c

STRUCTURAL ISSUES & REPAIRS

Structural issues should be addressed and surface treatments completed before reweaving. Woodworking repairs take a combination of skill, tools and courage. Get to know a local woodworker to act as your safety net. Our structural mantra: "There's nothing we can screw up that Bob (our structural guru) can't fix!" We are not, and don't claim to be, woodworking experts. We strive for functional repairs that blend in with the chair.

TOOLS AND MATERIALS

Far from an all-inclusive list, the following tools and materials are what we use most often.

Howard Feed-N-Wax: The orange oil nourishes dry wood and the beeswax gives you a protective layer. Apply with 000 or 0000 steel wool, or use soft cloth for shiny finishes. Allow 10-15 min to soak into the wood. Wipe off excess with a soft cloth. Light abrasion from steel wool blends scratches, removes oil/dirt buildup and paint splatter.

Tung Oil: 100% tung oil without extra drying elements is preferable. Works best when applied to raw wood. Provides a waterproof, hard finish. We use one coat of undiluted tung oil for most applications. Apply with 000 or 0000 steel wool. Allow 10-15 min to soak into the wood. Wipe off excess with a soft cloth. Make sure you go back and wipe several times. The oil tends to weep out of the wood and if left to cure, makes for a sticky, waxy mess.

Carnauba/Bees/Ebony Wax: A clear wax coat provides additional protection if you are concerned about watermarks or ghosting a shiny finish. Ebony wax applied to joints or turnings provides a "shadow" effect that blends new repairs with aged frames. Apply with a soft cloth, let dry until opaque and buff off excess with a soft cloth.

Wood Glue: A standard yellow glue works for most applications. Occasionally, we use a water-resistant or waterproof glue if moisture is a concern. Apply with a brush or inject into cracks using a syringe.

Hide Glue: We use hide glue primarily when we are working with historically significant chairs. Hide glue is great if you are looking for a 100% reversible bond. Titebond makes a premixed/squeeze bottle version that suits our purposes.

Cyanoacrylate (CA) Glue—Thin: A powerful solution for endless

STRUCTURAL ISSUES & REPAIRS (CONTINUED)

applications. The water-thin variety wicks into cracks and joints that can't be spread apart easily. Drip on the glue using the applicator tip, watch it disappear into the crack or joint and wipe up excess with a DRY paper towel. Moisture cures this glue so a wet paper towel will cure it immediately, leaving a nasty white residue and blocking the area from additional glue application. The glue heats up when it cures. If you spill and wipe up a puddle with the paper towel, the towel might smolder, but we've never had it catch flame.

Debonder: It's worth the extra investment just in case you glue your fingers together or to something important.

Accelerant: For small chips or unclampable situations, it's nice to have a way to force curing immediately. Available in spray and aerosol varieties. We use this stuff sparingly because it smells awful and we want to keep as many brain cells as possible. Be careful because the accelerant can damage finishes.

Epoxy—Structural: Use a high strength epoxy in areas missing too much material for a wood glue bond. We use a five-minute, quick-cure variety. Mix enough to cover all necessary surfaces and be ready with the clamps!

Epoxy—Filler: Use an epoxy putty stick for patching missing wood. The Mohawk product that we use is shapeable by hand, carvable with a chisel/blade and sandable. It comes in a large variety of colors, but we primarily use walnut, oak and maple. Get close to the tone of the wood, then add color once the epoxy is cured and shaped. Only mix what you need, because it becomes unworkable in five minutes or so. Apply excess epoxy and then carve it back to the shape you want. The outer surface of the cured epoxy is shiny and doesn't take color very well. It's also impossible to get the "perfect" shape by hand.

Wood Filler: If a crack is too small for the epoxy putty, we use a water-based wood filler. Do yourself a favor and spend a little extra on the good stuff with a finer texture.

TransTint: For coloring matching wood and epoxy/filler patches, we use a concentrated dye from TransTint. It comes in a wide variety of colors, but we primarily use golden brown, honey amber, dark walnut, and red mahogany. Colors can be mixed, diluted with water or denatured alcohol and a few drops go a long way. This product is extremely forgiving. Wipe off excess immediately for a light application or let it sit for a darker color. If you screw up you can usually remove most of the color by immediately wiping the area with a wet rag. Be aware that TransTint does not get along well with oils and waxes. Add color first and then use oil/wax.

Clamp—Ratchet Strap: A standard 1" ratchet strap is a tool with more applications then you could ever imagine. The straps are relatively soft on chair frames, you have great control over the clamping pressure and you aren't locked into clamping in a straight line like a bar clamp.

Clamp—Threaded Bar Clamp: We use a variety of sizes from 6" to 24" depending on the application. The best part is the ability to finely control the clamping pressure. Bonus: Bar clamps are great as pseudo-chair legs for removable seats.

Handscrew-style Wood Clamp: These are infinitely adjustable and great when you need to clamp at a weird angle or need to clamp a large area.

Spreader: A "reversible" clamp is super helpful when removing arms and disassembling chairs to replace stretchers. Many quick-clamps have the ability to become spreaders. Move the small jaw from one side of the clamp to the other and you've got a spreader instead of a clamp.

Rubber Mallet/Dead-Blow Hammer: Invaluable when knocking joints apart. The impact breaks dry glue joints free.

Cabinet Scrapers: Square or curved metal cards. Great for scraping glue and fine-tuning patches. Leaves the surface less porous than sandpaper and material removal is more precise.

Other Odds and Ends: Rasp, glue syringe, glue brush, 000 or 0000 steel wool, sandpaper (variety of grits), paper towel, soft cloth rags.

STRUCTURAL REPAIR CHECKLIST

When a chair enters the shop, run through this inspection/repair list to prepare the chair for weaving.

1 **Remove old seat:** Refer to the appropriate project section for detailed instructions.

2 **Wipe down frame:** If the frame is extremely dirty, you may want to use a mild soap solution. Wipe off excess water from the frame with a soft, dry rag. Be aware that some finishes will react badly or leave watermarks—it's always best to test on a hidden area of the finish.

3 **Address stretcher issues:** Both rails that support the seat and rungs that don't. (See Skill: Addressing Stretcher Issues on the next page.)

4 **Glue loose joints:** The best method is to spread the joints apart, clean the area, introduce wood glue and clamp the chair back together. That said, it can be extremely time consuming and often damaging to knock a chair completely apart using spreader clamps, mallets and solvents.

Most chairs aren't historically significant and can take advantage of the wicking properties of water-thin CA glue. Put the chair on a flat work surface→place a strap clamp around the legs of the chair→tighten until chair feels solid (keep the ratchet in between the legs to avoid damaging the wood)→if the chair rocks diagonally after tightening the initial strap clamp use another clamp or bungee to pull the floating legs toward each other→slowly drip CA glue into the top of every joint until the glue begins to pool at the bottom of the joint or drips down the leg→wipe up excess glue→wait for glue to cure overnight before removing strap clamp.

Be methodical when regluing so that you don't miss any joints. Apply glue to all the joints on one side of the chair, rotate to the next side, etc.

PRO TIP:
Tenon Cutters

If you find yourself doing many stretcher replacements, it's worth investing in tenon cutters. They are available for tapered shoulders and hard shoulders as a drill attachment or hand tool.

4

STRUCTURAL REPAIR CHECKLIST (CONTINUED)

SKILL // ADDRESSING STRETCHER ISSUES

Bowed Seat Rail

Replace if the bow is extreme or feels structurally unsound. If the bow is slight, you can try spinning the rail so that the bow is facing outward. If it won't spin, you can live with it or choose to replace it.

Broken Seat Rail

Must be replaced for structural stability. The length of the replacement rail includes the visible rail and both tenons.

Removal:

1. Measure and record the length of the exposed rail. [A]
2. Cut broken rail at both posts.
3. Drill a small pilot hole in the center of the remaining tenon.
4. Enlarge the hole. You can usually feel when the bit cuts through the old tenon and into the pocket at the bottom of the mortise.
5. Use a small chisel/pick to chip the remaining parts of the tenon out of the mortise.

Prepare new rail:

1. Measure and record depth of both mortises
2. Subtract ~⅛" from each mortise measurement and record as tenon lengths. [B & C]
3. Add both tenon lengths to the exposed rail length recorded previously for a total rail length.

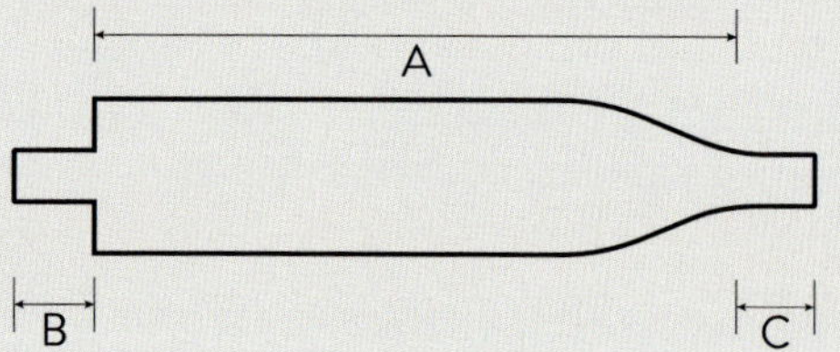

4. Choose a dowel the same width as the broken rail.
5. Cut dowel at total rail length.
6. Mark tenon lengths on each end of the dowel.
7. Shape new tenons and test-fit as you go. Aim for a fit that is snug, but hand-removable.

Rub-marks where the tenon hits the mortise show where material needs to be removed.

Tapered shoulder:

Hand-shape tenon and shoulder using whatever combination of blade, chisels, rasp, and sandpaper that you have available. Calipers are helpful, but not necessary.

Hard shoulder:

1. Make a shallow saw cut at the tenon length mark.
2. Start shaping tenon by removing material up to that mark.
3. Increase saw cut depth and continue the process until desired fit is achieved. Using whatever combination of blade, chisels, rasp and sandpaper that you have available. Calipers are helpful, but not necessary.

Installation:

1. Use spreader in between posts.
2. Brush glue on both tenons and mortises.
3. Fit new rail.
4. Clamp.
5. Wipe up excess glue.
6. Let dry overnight.
7. Color/oil/wax as necessary.

Broken Rung (Not broken seat rail)

It's usually best to replace a broken rung. (Refer to Broken Seat Rail for instructions.) Sometimes that would include difficult color matching, potential damage from chair disassembly or turnings that would require a lathe and turning skills. If that's the case, a repair is an option.

Repair a wood grain split:

1. Spread broken area apart using a spacer or spreader.
2. Brush wood glue onto both sides of the break.
3. Clamp.
4. Leave overnight.
5. Clean up glue.
6. Color/oil/wax as necessary.

Repair a cross-section break:

1. Spread broken area apart using a spreader.
2. Drill a small pilot hole to a ¾"-1" depth in the center of both sides of the break.
3. Expand pilot hole until ~½ the size of the rung.
4. Select a hardwood dowel that will fit loosely in the drilled hole.
5. Cut dowel to dry fit and allow the joint to come together cleanly.
6. Fill both holes with high strength epoxy.
7. Clamp the repair.
8. Clean up epoxy drips.
9. Leave overnight.
10. Clean up excess epoxy.
11. Color/oil/wax as necessary.

Cross-section break (left); wood grain split (right).

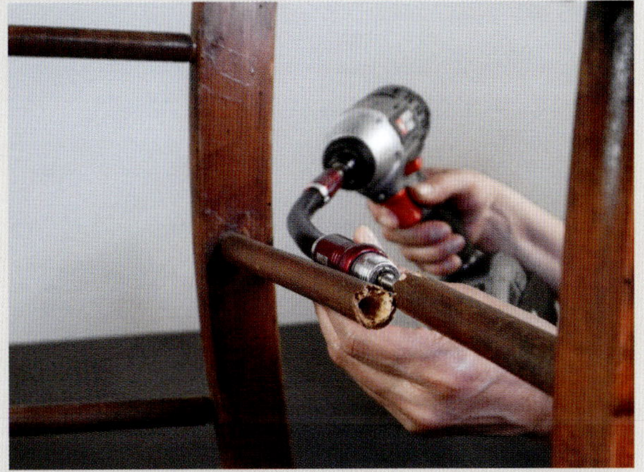

A flexible drill extension is helpful.

STRUCTURAL REPAIR CHECKLIST (CONTINUED)

5 **Glue broken bits and cracks:** Use wood glue if a piece is entirely broken off or you can spread a crack apart and clamp easily. CA glue is best for hairline cracks and difficult clamping areas.

6 **Patch missing wood and cracks:** Epoxy filler is best for large areas that need to be structurally stable or shaped to match carvings. Fill small cracks with wood filler.

7 **Color Match:** Use TransTint to blend patches and scratches.

5a

5b

6

7

8

8 **Clean and seal the finish:** We primarily use Feed-N-Wax to clean, nourish, and protect finishes. The abrasion of the steel wool and the lubrication of the oil blends scratches, blends watermarks, and removes most paint flecks. We avoid using steel wool on shiny finishes and use a soft cloth instead. Don't oil/wax the seat rails or they will be super slippery. Let it be known that we are far from claiming to be "finishing" experts. If you have concerns about a particular finish or product, consult a knowledgeable woodworker or the product manufacturer.

9 **Sharp edges:** Rectangular rails (and sometimes hand carved/aerofoil rails) have sharp edges. Take a rasp or sandpaper and roll those edges over to help extend the life of your new seat.

9a before

9b easing in progress

SPECIAL CASES—DISASSEMBLY REQUIRED

HITCHCOCK & WINDSOR

The disassembly and reassembly process is similar for both Hitchcock and Windsor chairs. The goal is to remove all parts of the chair frame that block access to the rails. It's possible to remove the original seat and weave through the slots left behind, but it's only worth the effort if the chair is truly crumbling and impossible to disassemble. If you break anything during the disassembly or reassembly process, please refer to common repairs outlined earlier in this section. Note that a spindle can usually be repaired like a rung.

DISASSEMBLY

Remove plugs/dowels: Wood plugs usually mask a screw, but occasionally there isn't a screw and what looks like a plug is actually a structural dowel. Either way, they need to be removed.

Use an awl to mark the center of the plug→Drill a small hole through the plug at the awl mark (you can usually feel the cavity/screw behind the plug) → expand the hole with larger drill bits (be careful not to damage the screw underneath) →clean away the rest of the plug using a small chisel or awl.

Dowels are more common on Windsor chairs than Hitchcock chairs and they can be located at a couple of different angles.

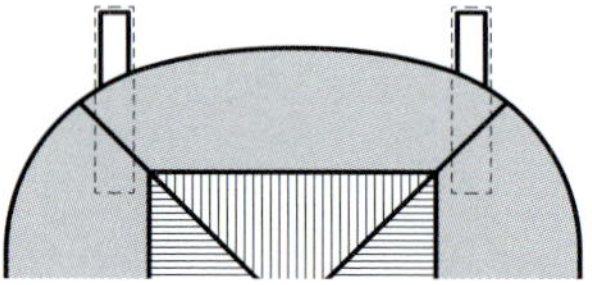

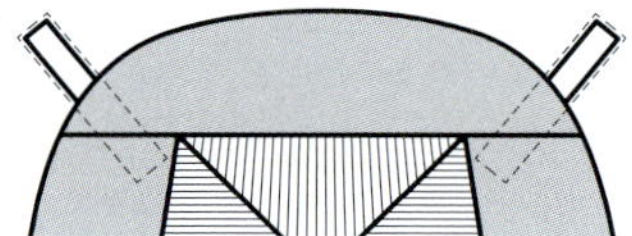

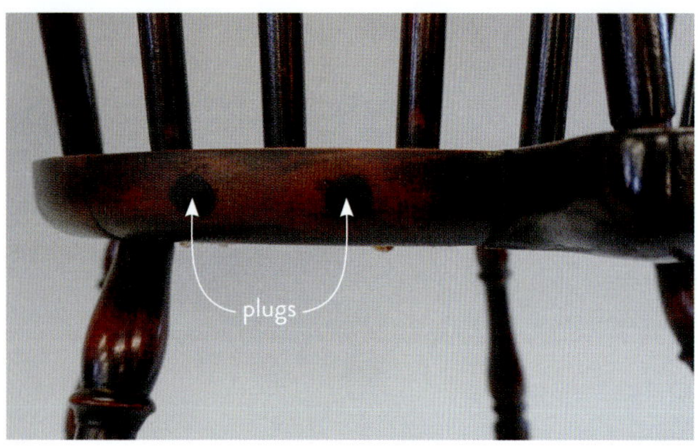

Follow the wall of the dowel hole with a small chisel→drill a small ¾"-deep hole at the angle of the wall→expand the hole with a larger drill bit→clean out excess material with a chisel/awl while continuing to follow the walls of the original hole→ repeat until dowel is fully removed. This is a painstaking process, so be patient and chip away a little at a time.

Remove screws: Clean glue/material out of the screw head with an awl→remove screw (this will often take any leftover material with it) →wrap screw with masking tape and write screw location on the tape for easier assembly later. A sealable bag tied to the frame is a great way to keep track of hardware.

Remove arms (as needed): Use a spreader and mallet to knock joints apart. Don't forget to remove plugs and screws first.

Remove skirts/wooden edges: Start with a stiff putty knife and pry between the skirt and the rush→expand the gap with a screwdriver→expand the gap more with a wooden wedge. Note that Hitchcock skirts are fragile and often pockmarked with nail holes from old removal/replacements. Be careful of rusty, broken-off nails. For Windsor chairs especially, you may need the impact of a rubber mallet to break apart glue joints.

REASSEMBLY (AFTER WEAVING NEW SEAT)

Repair or replace broken pieces: Use epoxy, wood glue or CA glue according to application and use repair instructions above. If a piece is beyond salvaging, work with a competent woodworker to have it manufactured.

Reglue joints: Clean up glue joints with a chisel/sandpaper→apply wood glue to both sides of the joint→clamp until screws/nails are in place.

Replace screws: Use the handy masking tape labels and reinstall screws in their original locations.

Replace nails: The thin Hitchcock skirts are nailed onto the rails. Drill new pilot holes and don't try to reuse old holes. Carefully set nails below the surface of the wood.

PRO TIP: *Plug Cutter*

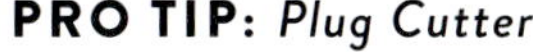

If you use a dowel for plugs, you will see end grain and that can take color differently than the edge/face grain. A plug cutter allows you to cut the required size plug from the edge/face grain of a board. This allows you to better match the grain of the chair frame and the plug will blend in more easily.

Replace plugs/dowels: Use the size dowel that fits snug in the empty hole→cut the plug/dowel to length so that ~½" is sticking out of the hole→apply glue to dowel and hole→hammer plug/dowel into place→let glue dry overnight→cut off excess dowel with a flush cut saw (be careful not to cut into the chair frame)→remove extra dowel material until flush with surface using a sharp chisel/sandpaper/steel wool.

Patch plugs/nails/cracks: Apply wood filler→let dry→smooth with sandpaper/steel wool.

Color match: Use TransTint for stained chairs. Get a paint match at your local hardware store for painted chairs.

WEAVING METHODS & MATERIALS

Rush chair

Warp/weft chair

The craft of chair seat weaving is so diverse that it is impossible to describe every variation of material and pattern. The instructions in this book cover common seat weaving processes. We introduce you to more advanced materials and give you a jumping off point for weaving. There is a lot of information and it can be confusing ... for instance, "rush" is both a weaving pattern and a weaving material. The rush pattern starts at the posts and works its way to the center of the seat, leaving a telltale series of triangles that meet in the center.

Chairs can also be woven in a warp/weft method (think loom weaving). The WARP strands are wrapped around the front and back rails, side by side as the base for weaving. The WEFT is woven over and under the warp strands around the side rails. You can also weave the opposite way, wrapping the warp side to side and weaving front to back. Basically, the warp is the foundation, and the weft is woven through the warp.

Cords can be woven in both the rush pattern and the warp/weft pattern. They encompass a wide range of materials including twisted paper products (Paper Rush, Danish Cord), hand-twisted plant fibers (Bulrush, Cattails, Corn Shucks) and other manufactured products (Pre-twisted Natural Rush, Twisted Seagrass.)

Flat materials, including splints, binder cane, and Shaker tape, are almost always woven in the warp/weft method. They can be woven in simple or ornate patterns. In the case of Shaker tape and flat-braided yarn, the color combinations are endless.

Cords

Pre-twisted Natural Rush

Paper Rush

Danish Cord

Hand-twisted Corn Shucks

Flat Materials

Splint Reed

Hickory Bark

Binder Cane

Shaker Tape

CHANGE IT UP

A chair with four rails can be woven with any number of materials. If you have a set of chairs, you could use a different material on each chair—or mix and match a set of Shaker tape chairs with different colors and patterns on each chair seat. The possibilities are endless!

Considering a new material for your chair:

- A trapezoidal seat with straight, round rails accommodates almost anything.
- Square rails work well with cords and Shaker tape, but not splint reed, binder cane or bark/wood splints.
- Curved rails aren't great for flat materials unless the curve is shallow or the material is narrow.
- Slots in the frame are tricky and usually work best with cords or Shaker tape.
- Shaker tape is a very beginner-friendly material.
- Practice with paper rush before attempting natural rush, and practice with splint reed before working with bark.
- Hitchcock and Windsor chairs that were originally rushed should probably stay rushed to keep the overall aesthetic.
- Honor the Danish cord or rattan material choices on Mid-Century designs.
- Not every chair could/should be woven. Often, chairs meant to be upholstered have very deep and narrow "rails." Technically this is a structure and not a "rail" and it is meant to support an upholstered base.
- Be creative in your material choices. Try paracord or upcycling neckties and belts. Make your own cords out of scrap fabric and weave in a rush pattern or in a warp/weft method.

Brandy Clements

Space-dyed Splint Reed in Diamond Pattern

David Klingler

Shaker Tape in X-Pattern

Becca Van K

Macrame Style Chairs

Sue Muldoon/Redux for You

Leather Straps in Plain Weave

David Klingler

Braided Cotton Cord in Greek Key Pattern

PROJECTS

SHAKER TAPE PROJECT

// TIME: ~2-4 HOURS //

Shaker tape is cotton strapping woven on a loom. It is produced in a variety of colors and with stripes. It is primarily available in 1" and ⅝" widths, though historically it was slightly wider and sometimes made with wool and dyed with natural materials. It was developed as a practical solution to wooden splint seats which dry out over time and could snag loose clothing. Traditionally two colors are woven together in a checkerboard pattern, but the design possibilities are infinite.

Shaker tape chairs emerged in the early 1830s, designed and built by the religious sect of the same name. The Shakers strive for practicality and simplicity in all aspects of life and are known for expressing those standards in their furniture. 1820-1865 is considered the golden era of Shaker furniture production, but authentic Shaker chairs from any era are highly collectable. Shaker influences are found in the work of many famous furniture designers, including Charles Eames, Gustav Stickley, and Hans Wegner.

Today, Shaker Workshops in Sandwich, N.H., carries on the tradition under the stewardship of Tappan Chair Company, a 200-year-old New England tradition in and of itself. Tappan Chairs has given a nearly 25% ownership stake to the living Shaker Community of Sabbathday Lake Shakers to honor their legacy.

A Warp and Weft Method is used for weaving Shaker tape. The warp wraps around opposing rails. The weft (or weaver) is woven through the warp strands. Typically, padding is added in between the layers of Shaker tape for structural support. Upholstery foam is a good option or, if you want to be very traditional, glue a fabric sheath to the rails and fill it with plant fibers or fabric.

Image courtesy of Shaker Village of Pleasant Hill

Heirloom Flamestitch.

Contemporary Flamestitch.

Refer to Materials, Tools & Skills Library for more detailed information.

**** Denotes tools that are helpful, but optional.***

TOOLS

Measuring Tape

Felt-tip Marker

Spring Clamp

Needle-nose Pliers

Flathead Screwdriver

Scissors

Hammer

"Ramp" Tool (butter knife, putty knife)

Nail Set*

Round Caning Needle*

MATERIALS

Shaker Tape ⅝" or 1" width

Upholstery Foam or Cotton Batting

Steel Tacks

Masking Tape

Thread

BASIC SKILLS

Sizing Foam

Using a Ramp

Inchworm Technique

Clamping

Tacking

Compressing on the Rails

Shaker tape of various widths, colors, and fibers from several different vendors.

Size: Shaker tape is commonly available in ⅝" and 1" widths. 1" tape is quick to weave. ⅝" tape lends itself to more intricate weaving patterns and results in a more solid seat.

Color: When choosing colors, consider that dark colors can fade in sunlight. Using the same color for warp and weft highlights the texture of the pattern while contrasting colors emphasize the pattern itself. If using two different colors, use the darker color for the warp. It is less likely to show dirt at the front rail where most of the wear happens.

Amount: Detailed calculations are found on the next page. Round up to the nearest five yards to avoid running out of material. If you have to order more tape, you'll pay additional shipping charges and risk color variations due to dye lot differences. Better to have more material than not enough. Seventy-five-yard rolls are much more cost effective when there is the potential for doing multiple projects.

Chair Frame: Any chair with 4 round rails can be woven with Shaker Tape. Square rails are ok. Curved rails are not ideal.

PRO TIP

Pneumatic Stapler: To save time and effort, use a pneumatic stapler instead of tacks. We use an upholstery stapler that shoots a 23 gauge, 3⁄16" crown staple in varying leg lengths.

Slotted Mandrel: If you are doing a large quantity of Shaker tape weaving, a slotted mandrel can be extremely helpful. This drill bit will roll up the material much quicker and tighter than you can by hand ... and it's mesmerizing to watch.

BEFORE YOU WEAVE

Take a photo of the old chair seat! It's fun to see before and after images. You may not want to use the old seat as a guide—the person before you could have made mistakes.

Remove the old seat. If you are interested in reusing the old material for seat weaving or another project, unweave and remove the Shaker tape carefully. You can wash the material and weave with the unfaded side out. This is especially helpful if you are dealing with Shaker tape that is no longer commercially available.

Otherwise, it's easiest to remove the seat using a good pair of scissors. Cut along the inside of the rails or wherever you can work the scissors into the pattern. Remove any tacks/staples in the rails. If you can't remove them, hammer them flush.

Address structural issues. [Refer to Structural Issues & Repairs]

Prepare the chair frame. Wipe down the frame to remove dirt and debris. Nourish the wood with oil and protect with wax.

Cut foam to size. To reduce the risk of seeing foam along the rails or in the corners at the posts, cut it about ½" smaller than the opening. Then cut 1" off each corner. [Refer to Materials, Tools & Skills Library]

SKILL // DETERMINE AMOUNT OF MATERIAL NEEDED

Determine the following measurements to the closest ½".

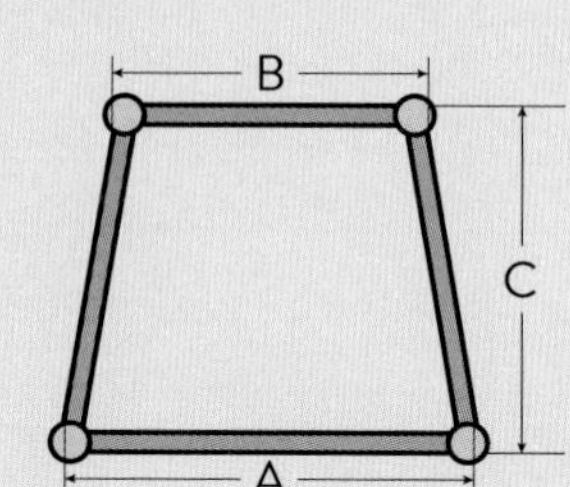

A: The width from the outside of the side rails behind the front posts.

B: The width from the outside of the side rails in front of the back posts.

C: The depth from the outside of the front rail to the outside of the back rail

Estimate the woven area. The measurements below reflect the project chair in this book.

Trapezoidal Seat

$$\frac{A+B}{2} \times C = \text{appropriate area estimate}$$

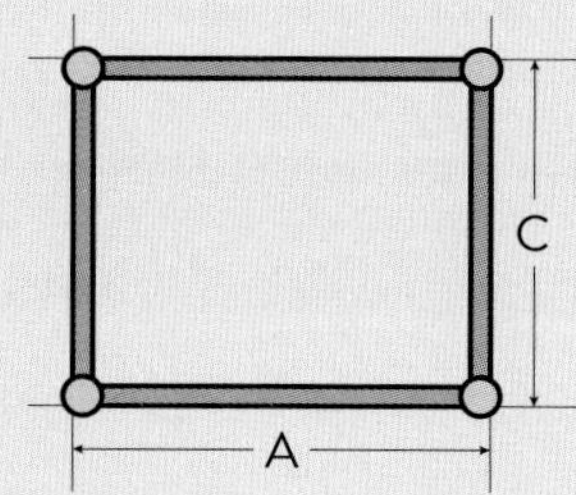

Example: A=20.5"; B=17"; C=17"

$$\frac{20.5+17}{2} \times 17 = 318.75$$

Rectangular Back or Barstool

A × C = Approximate Area

Example: A= 17"; C=12.5"   17" × 12.5" = 212.5 in^2

Divide your answer by one of the conversion factors below to determine the yards of tape required for the warp and the yards of tape required for the weft.

1" SHAKER TAPE: Divide by Conversion Factor of 18.
⅝" SHAKER TAPE: Divide by Conversion Factor of 11

Trapezoidal Seat

1" Shaker Tape	318.75 ÷ 18 = 17.7 yards; 20 yards of each color
⅝" Shaker Tape	318.75 ÷ 11 = 28.97 yards; 30 yards of each color

Rectangular Back

1" Shaker Tape	212.50 ÷ 18 = 11.8 yards; 15 yards of each color
⅝" Shaker Tape	212.50 ÷ 11 = 19.32 yards; 20 yards of each color

Note: If using the same color for warp and weft, multiply yardage by 2, so for this project ~40 yds of 1" or ~60 yds of ⅝" for the seat.

WRAP THE WARP

The warp is wrapped around opposing rails, typically front-to-back on a seat and vertically oriented on the back to follow any slight curve.

2

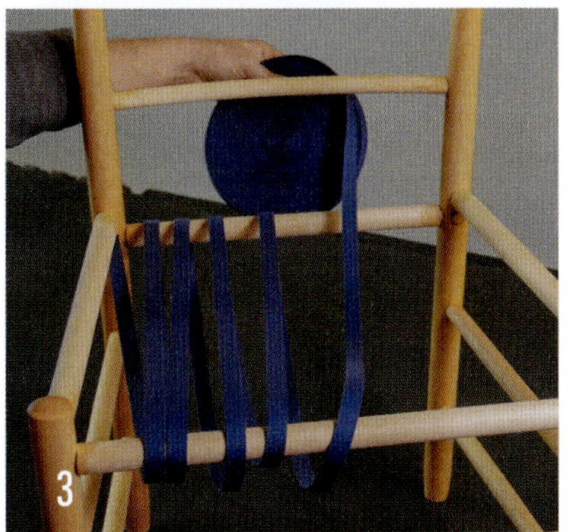
3

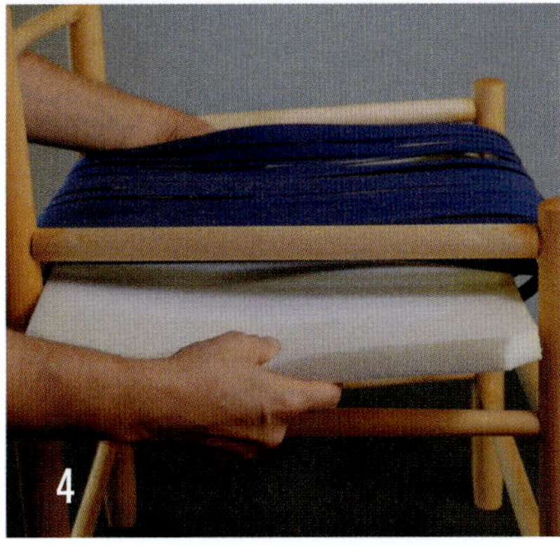
4

1 Roll up the material you are using for the warp. It's easier to wrap the rails from a roll than from a pile of tape. The weft tape can remain in a pile.

2 With the chair upside down, tack the loose end of the rolled warp tape to the left side rail at the back post.

3 Turn the chair upright, and bring the tape around front rail toward the back rail. Wrap loosely until you fill the back rail.

4 Insert the foam in between warp layers and check for twists in the warp strands.

SKILL // TACKING TIPS

[Refer to Materials, Tools & Skills Library]

Use an awl to make a pilot hole in material and/or rail.

Hold tack with needle nose pliers.

Use a nail set.

When securing Shaker tape with a tack on the top-side of a seat, make sure to tack on the inside of the rail and not directly on top of the rail.

WRAP THE WARP (CONTINUED)

5 Adjust the warp tension. Moving from the tacked end to the loose end, pull out the slack one strand at a time. Don't pull "tight," just remove the slack. When the warp is too tight, weaving is difficult. If you need to let go of the material, use a clamp on the rail to hold the tension. Before you move on to the next steps make sure the loose end is clamped securely.

6 Compress the material on the back rail to make sure that fill the rail completely. Use your fingers and/or a screwdriver. A slight buckling on the seat is OK, but don't let the strands overlap on the rail. If there isn't enough space for another strand, distribute the strands evenly along the rail.

7 Wrap the loose end around the front rail and toward the back post. Secure it with a tack on the inside of the right rail, approximately ½" from the back post.

8 Cut off the extra material approximately ¼" from the tack.

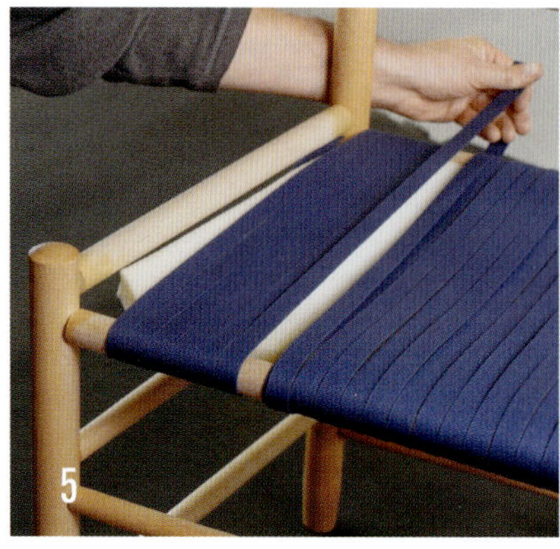

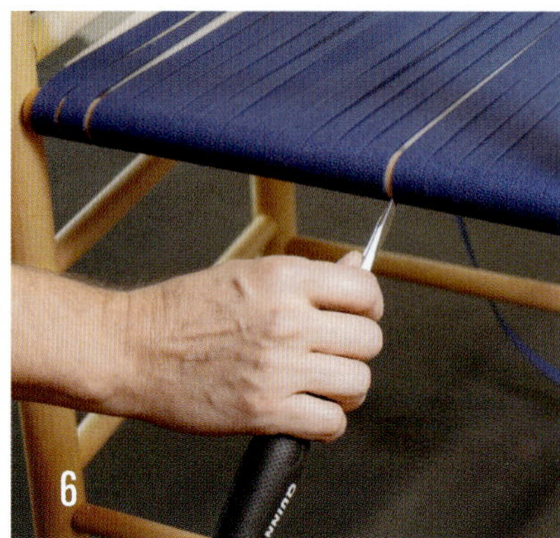

SKILL // WHERE TO CLAMP

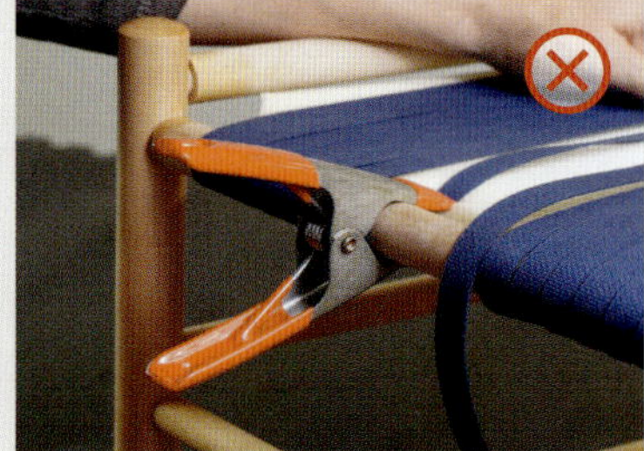

Clamping over rail adds slack into the pattern.

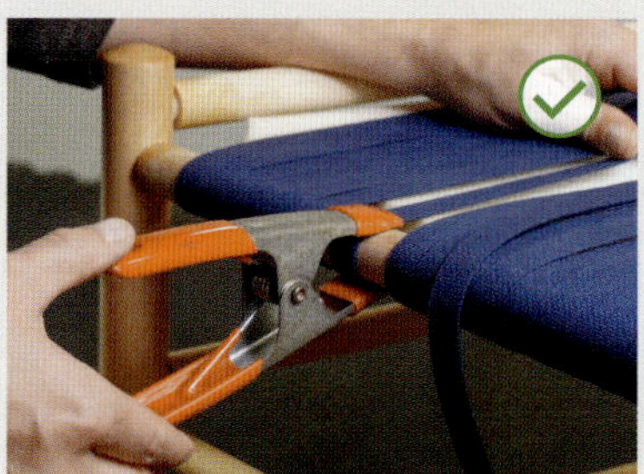

Clamping on rail holds tension firmly.

FILLING THE GUSSETS

EVERY CHAIR IS DIFFERENT! The goal when adding filler strands is to get the maximum amount of material on the front rail while keeping the warp perpendicular to the front/back rails. You may end up with three filler strands on each side, you may end up with one or you may end up with a different number on each side if your chair is asymmetrical. Squish strands together but don't overlap. If you don't have enough space for another filler, distribute the strands evenly along the front rail.

9a

9b

9c

9d

10

underside of chair seat at left side rail

9 Tack a filler strand to the right rail. Technically, the tack at the right rear post is the first of the filler strands on that side. The next filler strand starts to the right of that first strand. Don't forget to tack on the inside of the rail.

Place the tack so that the filler strand stays parallel to the rest of the warp. **[9b]**

Don't tack too close to the neighboring strand and create an overlap. **[9c]**

Don't tack too far away from the neighboring strand and leave a gap in the pattern. **[9d]**

10 Tack the filler strand on the bottom. Turn your chair upside down, ensure that the strand isn't twisted, pull the strand taut and tack the loose end of the strand ½" from the back post. Cut off excess material approx ¼" from the tack.

Keep filler strands parallel to the existing warp. It is more important to have the filler strands parallel on the top. Don't worry if the attached end is slightly splayed on the bottom. It will even out when you weave the seat.

FILLING THE GUSSETS (CONTINUED)

11 Add a filler strand to the left gusset. Tack the first filler strand to the inside of the side rail with a ½" gap off of the back post. Tack loose end of the filler strand on the bottom of the rail. Make sure the strand stays parallel to the existing warp. Cut excess material after securing the strand on the bottom.

12 Continue to add filler strands to both gussets until the maximum amount of material is on the rail. Push strands together using a screwdriver, but don't let them overlap. If there isn't enough space for another strand, distribute the strands evenly along the rail. Make sure the warp strands stay perpendicular to the front/back rails.

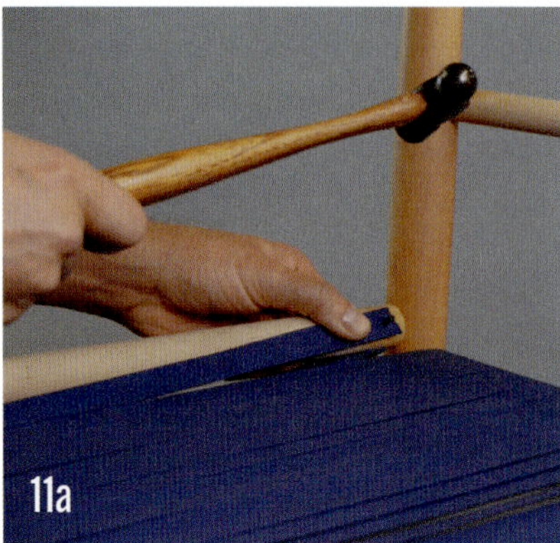
11a

11b

12

PRO TIP:

Make Space for Tacking

Use a clamp on the side rail to hold the warp strands out of your way when placing gusset tacks.

WARP THE BACK

Warp strands on a back are usually aligned vertically to account for any curvature in the top/bottom rails. We find it easier to work with the chair seat facing away from us.

- Tack the loose end of the rolled, warp material to the left post, ~1" above the bottom rail.
- Wrap the coil loosely around the top/bottom rails, check for twists in the material and then insert the foam in between the layers.
- Adjust the warp tension. Moving from the tacked end to the loose end, pull out the slack one strand at a time.
- Compress the strands to together on the rails to add wraps. A slight buckling of the strands is acceptable, but don't let them overlap.
- Secure the loose end with a tack on the back side of the upright rail, ~1" below the top rail. Cut off the extra material ~¼" from the tack.

Note: The warp strands will be at a slight angle on the back side. This is normal and necessary for the strands on the front to stay perpendicular to the rails.

TOP RAIL LONGER THAN THE BOTTOM RAIL:

If the top rail is a strand width or more longer than the bottom rail, you need to end the wrap with a tack on the front side of the post. Refer to FILLING THE GUSSETS if you have extra space on the top rail once the bottom rail is full.

WEAVE THE WEFT

For this project, we weave the top in plain weave and the bottom in a 2-under/2-over twill. More complicated weaves (diamonds, chevrons, etc.) combine these two basic patterns. Pattern mapping skills and samples of advanced patterns can be found in the appendices. Note: The weaving skills required for the back are the same as the seat. Start on the bottom rail of the back side of chair back.

Seat bottom is woven in a 2-over/2-under twill pattern.

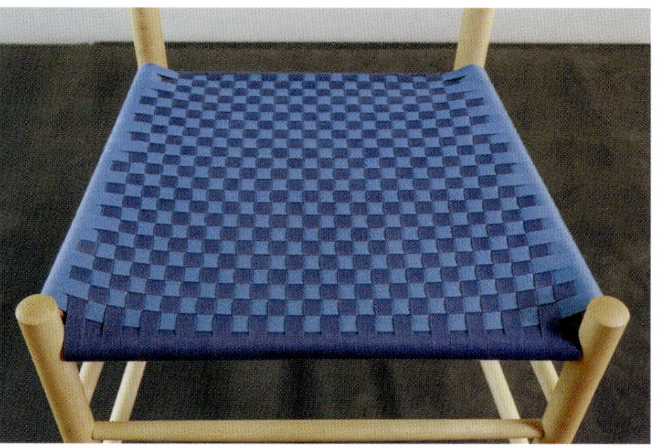

For this project, the seat top is woven in plain weave.

13 Weave the first row. The weaver end should hide under the leftmost warp strands on the front rail (chair seat) or bottom rail (chair back). Count the furthest left two warps as "under." Move to the right counting the next two warps "over," then 2-under/2-over, etc. You may end up with one warp strand at the opposite side. That is fine.

Count first, then weave so the end is hidden under warp strands.

14 Tack the weaver strand onto the front rail. Pry the warp strands apart, start the tack and use a nail set to tack flush. Flip the chair upright.

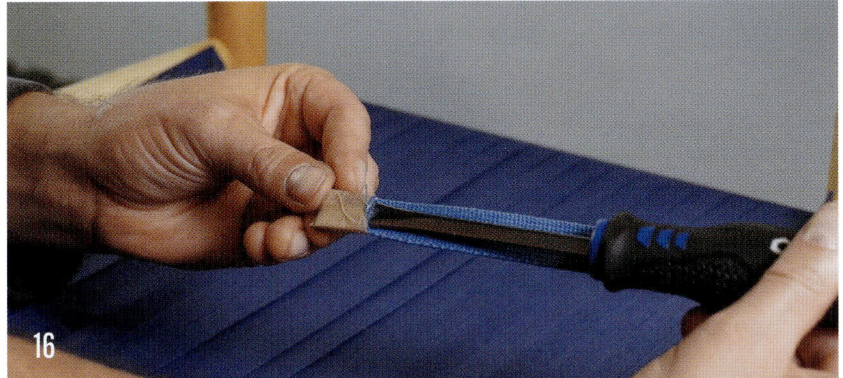
16

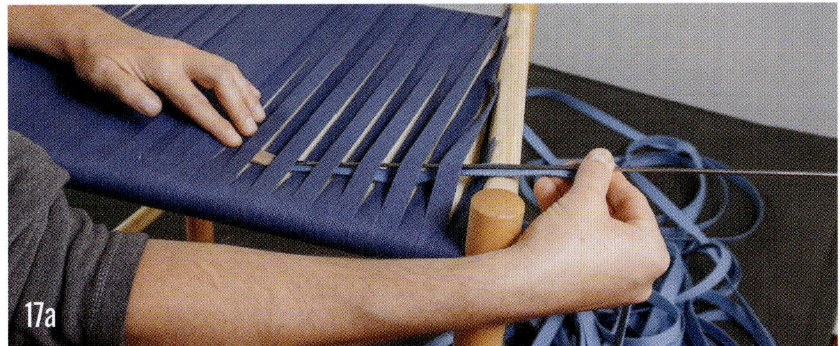
17a

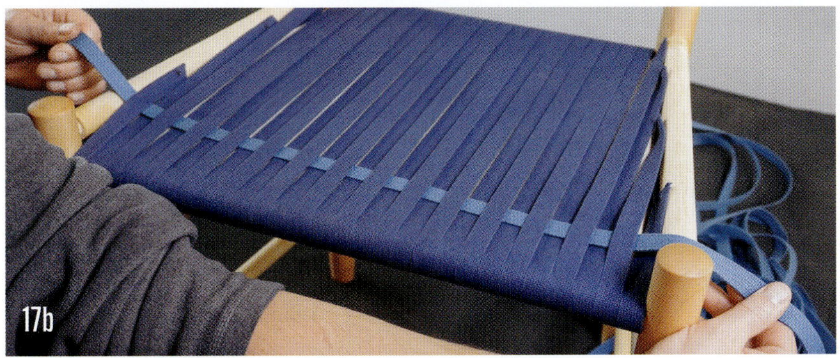
17b

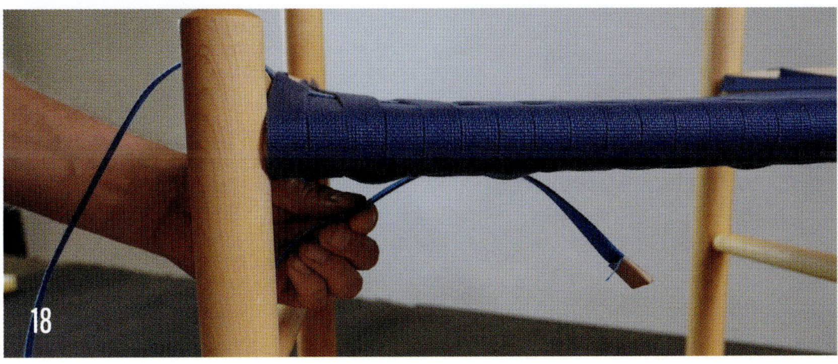
18

15 Determine the top and bottom of the weaving strand. You can't just grab the end and weave or you will have a twisty mess! Start where the weaver exits the bottom of the seat. Run your hand down the entire length of the weaver strand, removing twists. When you get to the end, tuck the tape (top side up) into the top of the pattern.

16 Make a weaving pocket. Turn the top end of the tape back on itself about ⅝" and wrap the pocket with tape.

The weaving pocket allows you to use a tool to push the weaver through the warp strands and also prevents fraying. The pocket should be on the outside or "top" of the weaver strand. Don't let the pocket drop once you've made it or you'll have to sort out top and bottom again.

17 Weave through the top of the seat in a 1-over/1-under pattern with the pocket side up. It doesn't matter whether you start "over" or "under." *Wait to pull slack.*

18 Tuck the pocket into the warp strands on the underside of the seat to keep the weaver untwisted. Pull the slack across the top of the chair from the right side to the left without pulling the pocket out of the bottom warp strands. Use maximum tension when pulling slack. It's not worth throwing your shoulder out, but make sure it's good and tight.

WEAVE THE WEFT (CONTINUED)

19 Turn the chair upside down and remove the pocket from the warp strands. Then weave the second row of the 2-over/2-under twill pattern on the bottom of the seat. The twill pattern is accomplished by backing up one warp strand for each weaver strand. The first weaver row started under two warp strands. The second weaver row will go under one warp strand and then continue 2-over/2-under. Do not pull slack yet.

19

20 Turn the chair upright and tuck the pocket into top of the seat. Now, pull the slack across the bottom of the chair from the left side to the right without pulling the pocket out of the top warp strands. Ergonomically, it's easier to pull slack with the chair upright.

21 Keep weaving until there are 3-4 rows on the top. After tensioning a row, push it close to the previous row on both the top and the bottom.

PRO TIP: *The Twill Pattern*

When the pattern develops, it looks like stairsteps. The effect is achieved by stepping the pattern back by one warp strand for each weaving row.

The pattern can get confusing at the rail. If you are having trouble determining where to go, look toward the center of the pattern. Use a short length of Shaker tape to simulate the pattern. Count back "2-over/2-under" to determine how to start weaving at the left rail.

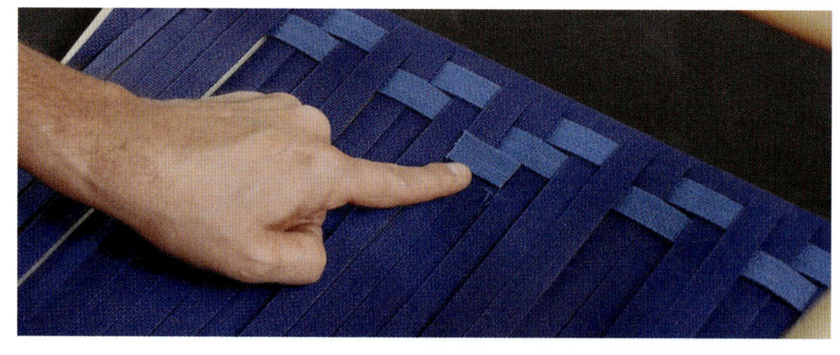

SKILL // ENCOUNTERING TACKS ON SIDE RAILS

Don't weave under a tacked warp strand if you have 1" or less between the tack and the previous weaver strand. Weaving under a strand too close to a tack results in a divot in the seat.

SKILL // COMPRESSING THE PATTERN

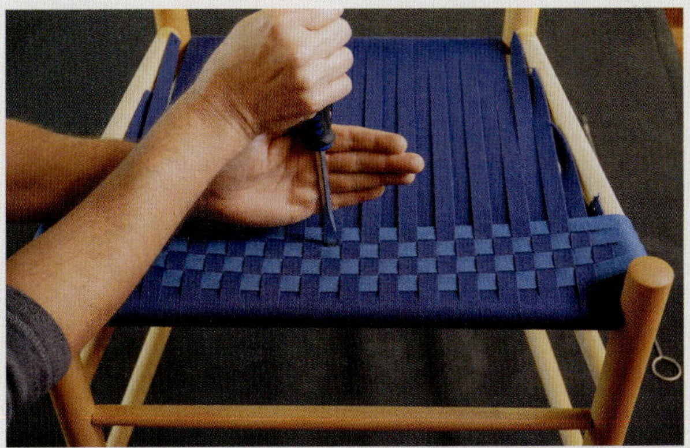

The goal is to get the most possible material on the seat and give yourself more room to weave at the end of the project. With loose patterns like twill, pushing the strands together by hand is enough. The checkerboard/plain weave is very tight, so compressing requires a tool. Start with the first row and bow it slightly toward the front rail. Use a flathead screwdriver like a paddle and pull the next row snug against the first. Work methodically from one one rail to the other. Continue compressing each row separately. Compress on the rails and within the pattern every few rows. You don't have to start back at the very front each time you adjust.

SKILL // USING A RAMP

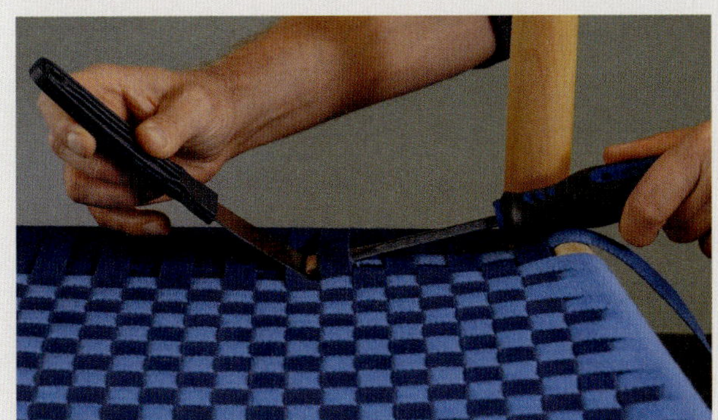

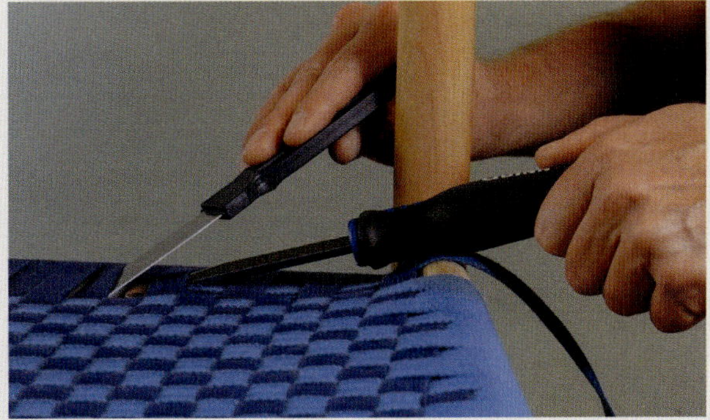

A ramp tool is not only easier on the hands, it's absolutely necessary as weaving progresses and warp strands tighten. Place the ramp at a steep angle where you want the weaver to exit the pattern. Push the weaver through the pattern and it will follow the ramp to exactly where you wanted it to go. As the pattern tightens, you can use the ramp to guide the weaver into the pattern as well.

WEAVE THE WEFT (CONTINUED)

22 Compress the pattern periodically throughout the weaving process.

23 Continue weaving top and bottom, pulling slack, tensioning, and compressing the pattern until the side rails are full. Ideally, all the strands will lay flat along the side rails, but it's OK if the last row is a little crumpled. If you can't make enough space for another strand, distribute the strands evenly along the side rail. For the last few rows, it may be easier to weave and pull slack on half a row at a time.

24 Weave the last row on the bottom, going as far as you can without changing the pattern. Pull the weaver strand up onto the back rail, pry the last "2-under" warp strands apart and tack the weaver onto the back rail. Use a tack set if you're concerned about damaging the material.

25 Cut the loose end of the weaver leaving a ½" tail. Tuck the tail inside the pattern and adjust the warp strands so that both the tail and tack disappear.

26 Give yourself a high-five or do a little dance! Give your seat a little drum tap, hug the chair, whatever feels good. The gratification of finishing a chair project never gets old.

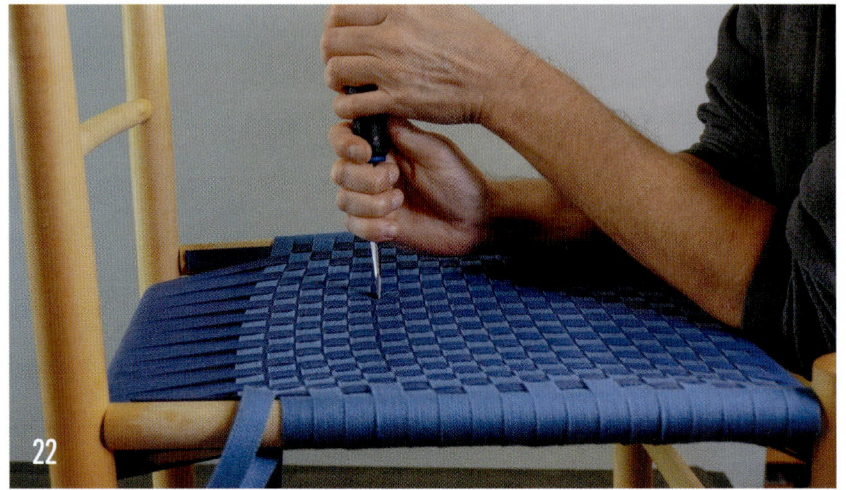
22

24a
bottom back rail

24b
bottom back rail

MAINTENANCE

Keep Shaker tape chairs indoors! Direct sunlight causes fading. Clean periodically with a vacuum. Spot-clean with a mild soap solution, but don't saturate the seat. Scotch guard is OK, but test a sample before spraying the whole seat.

SKILL // SPLICING STRANDS

If you run out of tape or decide to change colors mid-warp or mid-weft, you'll need to splice on a new strand. Do this by overlapping the new and old strands and sewing them together. We prefer to use a glover's needle (very sharp, use a thimble, don't bleed on your Shaker tape) and upholstery thread that matches the Shaker tape.

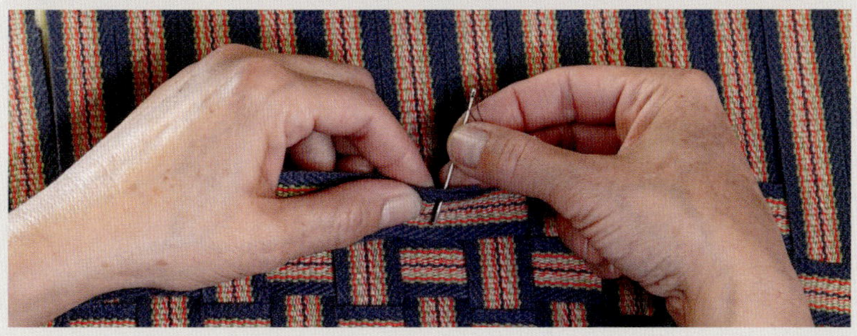

Mark the splice. Ideally the splice lies hidden "under" warp strands. Insert the new weaver strand under the old one, overlapping 2"-3". Sew along the mark using two rows of a simple straight stitch.

Splicing Rules:

- Always splice on the bottom.
- Always splice in the center of the seat at least 4" away from the rail.
- Don't trim too close to the stitches.

DESIGN TIPS

Simple frames are better. Slots are tricky, but not impossible. Straight rails are ideal, but slight curves are OK. Steep siderails cause the material to slip toward the back posts.

The material slips along convex or concave curves. It won't lay flat and gaps/bunching is inevitable.

Rail interruptions cause gaps in the weave.

SPLINT REED PROJECT

// TIME: ~3-6 HOURS //

Splint reed or flat reed is cut from the inner pith of the rattan palm. It is a manufactured substitute for the more laborious split oak, ash or hickory bark. Reed is processed into widths from 1" down to ¼" with slight variations in color and straightness. A natural light-tan color ages to a golden brown after a few years. Manufactured paper splint and smoked reed look more like bark. Dyed reed is fun to work with and gives the chair a vibrant makeover. You can purchase it already dyed or dye your own. Add a capful of Retayne color fixer to water when soaking. Be aware that some color will bleed out and may stain your clothing/towels/work surface. Binder cane, the cut of rattan that still has the shiny skin, can be woven in this way. It's tedious and slicey stuff, but it is really pretty and strong.

Splint chair seats are woven in a warp/weft method. Warp strands are typically wrapped around the front and back rails and provide the base for weaving. Weft strands weave over and under warp strands and around the side rails. We call the weft strands "weavers" to avoid confusion. The typical pattern is a twill weave, although by varying the weavers, diamonds and chevrons, and X patterns can make things fun. Checkerboard (1-over/1-under) is very hard to weave with splint reed. Despite finding splint reed on porch rocking chairs, it is best kept indoors.

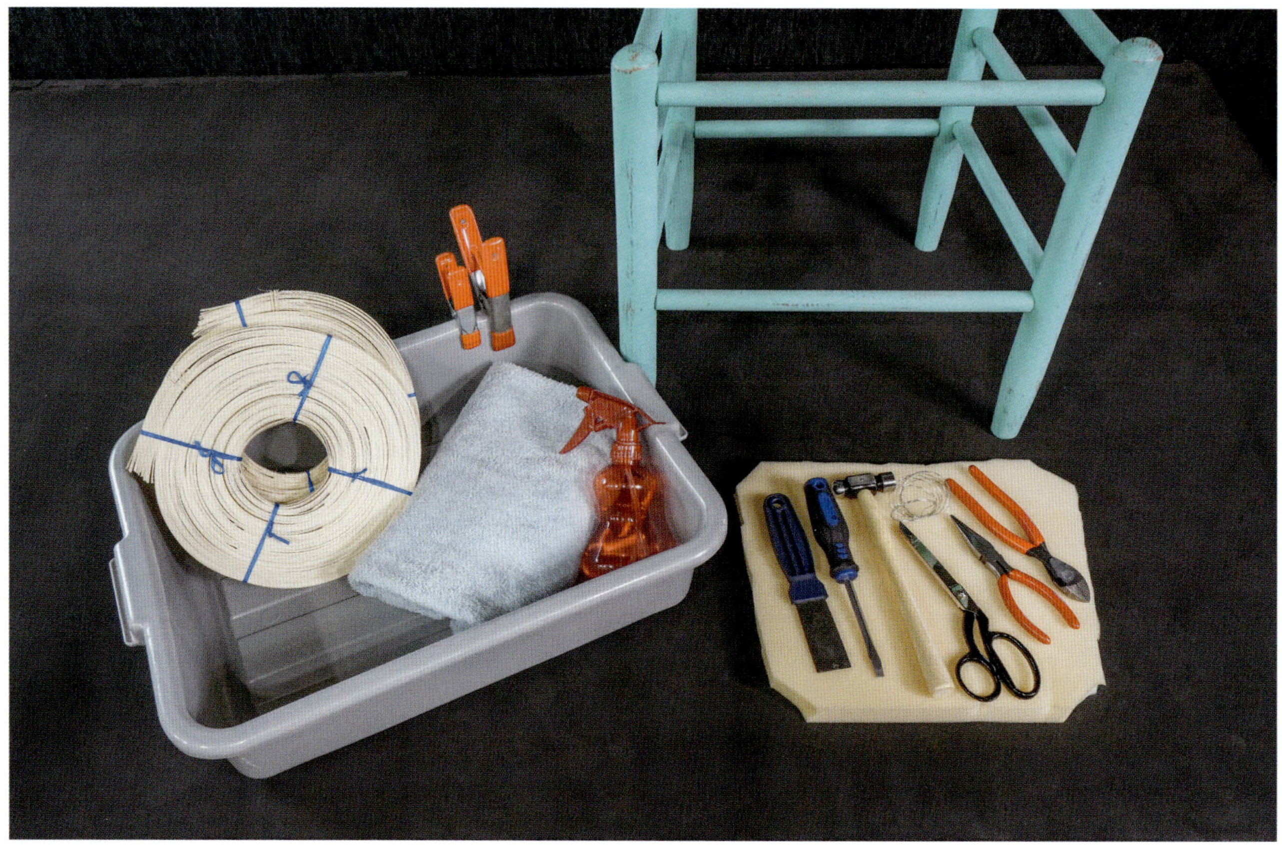

Refer to Materials, Tools & Skills Library for more detailed information.

**** Denotes tools that are helpful, but optional.***

TOOLS

Wire Cutter

Needle-nose Pliers

Spring Clamp

Scissors

"Ramp" (Butter Knife/Putty Knife)

Flathead Screwdriver

Hammer

Tub/Bucket

Towel(s)

Spray Bottle*

Paint Brush

MATERIALS

1 ½ - 2 lb Flat Reed

Wire

Upholstery Foam

Protective Coating (Shellac, Polyurethane, etc.)

BASIC SKILLS

Sizing Foam

Using a Ramp

Inchworm Technique

Clamping

Compressing on Rails

Apply Protective Coating

Flat Reed: We are using ½" flat reed that comes in a 1 lb coil. The average chair measures ~17" across the front rail. For that size, plan on using 1 ½ - 2 coils. Expect to have material left over, but that is better than running short. Be kind to the material: Clip loose fibers, don't pull them or you risk splitting the reed. The grain runs lengthwise and it will easily break along the grain (especially if you step on it). Don't bend the material back on itself or it will crack. Find the "Top" and "Bottom" of the material. The smoother, top side should face the outside of the seat. Bend reed into a U. Look for fibers popping up. Bend the other way. Whichever side has more fibers is the BOTTOM and should face INSIDE the seat. The chair won't fall apart if the reed is reversed. Sometimes it's hard to tell and you won't know until the seat dries. If fibers stick out on the rails, then you can trim or sand the fibers.

Chair Frame: Splint reed is best suited for weaving on post and rung chairs with round, straight rails. A rail height difference is a normal construction element. Older, handmade versions often have hand-sculpted "aerofoil" rails. Do not use splint reed on squared rails. Even with foam stuffing, the reed will easily break along the edges of the rails.

Fluffy Fibers—Go Inside.

Smooth Fibers—Go Outside.

Fluffy Fibers—Go Inside; Smooth Fibers—Go Outside.

Rectangular rails are not appropriate for splint reed—the material will break on the sharp edge.

BEFORE YOU WEAVE

Take a before photo of the chair! It's fun to see before and after. You may not want to use the previous seat as a guide—the previous weaver could have made mistakes.

Remove the old seat. Use a blade, snips, or scissors. If using a blade, cut along the inside of the rails; cutting on the rails can damage them. A sawing motion usually works best. Cut from the posts to the middle, rotating the chair around. This helps avoid accidentally cutting the post. Peel the material off of the rails and push the old material down. Remove any tacks/staples in the rails. If you can't remove them, hammer them flush.

Address structural issues. [Refer to Structural Issues & Repairs]

Prepare the chair frame. Wipe down the frame to remove dirt and debris. Nourish the wood with oil and protect with wax. We like Howard Feed-N-Wax or tung oil. Be very careful with shiny, lacquered finishes—don't use steel wool or wax. If in doubt, consult the manufacturer or a professional woodworker/furniture refinisher.

Cut foam to size. To reduce the risk of seeing foam along the rails or in the corners at the posts, cut it about ½" smaller than the opening and then cut 1" off each corner. [Refer to Materials, Tools & Skills Library]

Soak the Splint Reed. Clip the strings on one coil of reed. Keeping it loosely coiled, soak it in warm water for 15-20 minutes. Cover the reed with a hand towel to help submerge. (Note: If you don't cut the strings, the water will not penetrate to the inside of the coil.) Soaking too long or resoaking multiple times will discolor and compromise the material. It's best to only soak as much as you need at a time, which is rarely more than one coil.

Sort the Splint Reed by Lengths. Remove the reed and drain off excess water. Hold the ends and let the fibers fall. Separate short strands (< 4'-5'), loosely coil, and set aside on a towel. Pull a few longer strands. Coil remaining long/medium strands loosely-this will keep the cane from drying out.

Alternate using medium and longer strands throughout the process. You'll likely have more medium/short strands than long strands. If you use up all of your long strands at the beginning you will be splicing strands every time you weave a row at the end. Doubling up strands to splice at the end is extremely difficult.

WRAPPING THE WARP

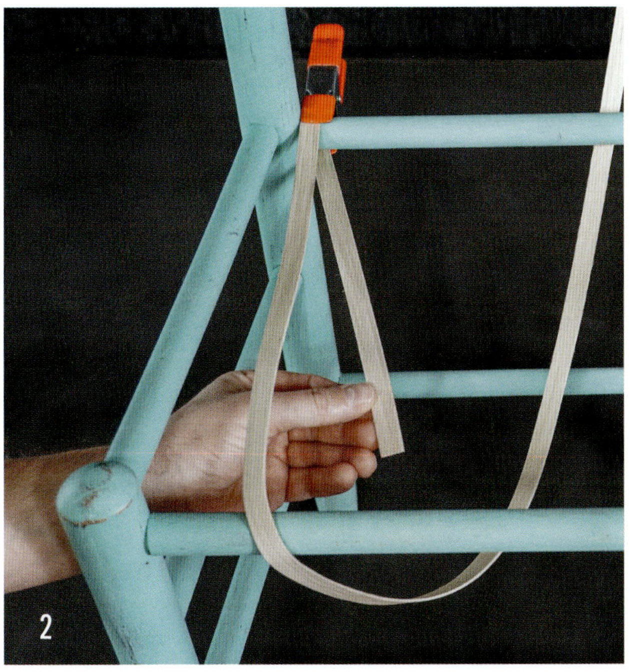

2

3

SKILL // TENSION

Proper tension can be tricky. Consider rail height differences. Too tight, and weaving is difficult. Too loose, and the seat will sag and the warp strands will bump out along the front rail.

Better to leave the warp slightly too loose than too tight. You can tighten loose warp strands throughout the process. Choose the middle path: Not maximum tension, not so loose the reed rides up on other warp strands. Keep in mind that splint reed does not shrink when drying.

1. Find the top side of a long strand of reed.

2. Bring one end of the reed across the top of the seat. Wrap it over and around the back rail and clamp on the back rail, leaving 8"-10" end. Bring the long end over and under the front rail.

3. Splice the strand to itself midway between front and back rails. [Refer to skill box on the next page.] The first and last warp strands will be these V-splices, where the reed joins to itself, becoming one strand. The reed should overlap roughly 4". Align the spliced loop perpendicular to the front/back rails.

WRAPPING THE WARP (CONTINUED)

SKILL // WHERE TO CLAMP

4 Continue to wrap the loose end of the strand up and around the back rail, toward you and under the front rail until you run out of material. Keep even tension.

5 Splice in a new strand. Cut off excess material from the original strand leaving roughly 4" between the end and the back rail. Check top and bottom of the new strand before splicing! Mid-warp splicing should have a roughly 2" tail on either side of the wire wrap.

SKILL // SPLICING WARP STRANDS

Practice wire wraps on short scrap strands. If the splice doesn't slip under tension, consider it a success!

1. Wet a new strand and shake off excess water. Find top and bottom.
2. Overlap the strands ~4". Start with the stabby end of the wire in the center of the strands at the midpoint of overlap.
3. Wrap the wire snuggly around both strands 3-4 times.
4. Cut off excess wire. Leave the stabby end in the center of the strands.
5. Gently pinch the wire wrap with pliers.

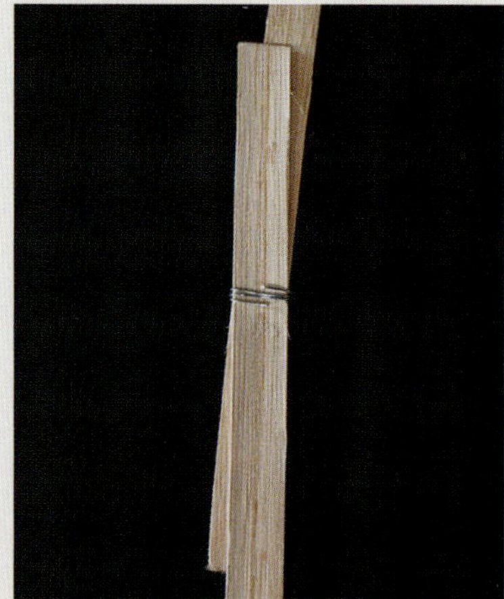

Warp Splicing Rules:

- Always splice on the bottom of the seat or the back of a chair back.
- Always splice at least 6" from the rail.

WARNING: Wire can make you bleed. "Oh I hate it when I bleed on the chair!" is a common refrain when seat weavers gather. Scientific experiments show that your own saliva is a good way to remove blood from reed.

6 Continue wrapping warp strands and splicing strands together until you fill the back rail with reed. On a trapezoidal seat, both sides of the front rail will be visible when the back rail is full.

7 Work the maximum amount of material onto the back rail. The strands may look like they're touching, but it's surprising how much cumulative space is available when you compress them together. If there isn't enough space for another strand, distribute the strands evenly along the rail. Use a flathead screwdriver or putty knife, being careful not to chip the reed. [Refer to Materials, Tools & Skills Library]

8 Splice the final warp strand to itself in a V-Splice. Clip excess reed leaving ~3" in case you need to adjust tension later. The bottom of the seat will be angled slightly so the top can be perpendicular. Any strands curving over each other will work their way out when weaving.

WRAPPING THE WARP (CONTINUED)

9 Test the tension and adjust if needed.

10 Clip corners of the foam and insert it between the warp layers. It is easiest to insert the foam from under the side rail. Be careful not to cut your hand on the wire wraps. Foam should "float" in the center, without touching the rails.

SKILL // TENSION ADJUSTMENT

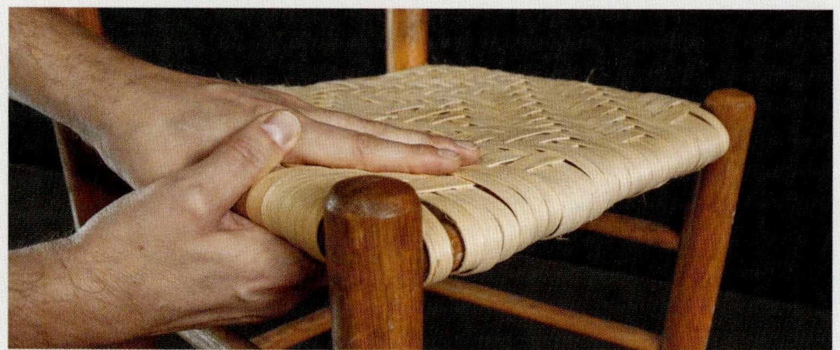

Sometimes tension issues don't show up until you are weaving. These methods can be used at any point in the process. Be patient finding wire wraps and work with care when pulling material through the woven strands.

Too Tight: If you can't work the foam between the layers easily, your warp is likely too tight. Wet the reed. Undo the final wire wrap and work slack toward the left. Re-tension working from left to right, moving splices so they stay on the bottom.

Too Loose: Place one hand on top and one hand underneath and press. Look along the front rail. If the strands push away from the front rail in an uneven way, you should add more tension to the warps.

Spritz the entire seat. Start at the initial wire wrap and tighten the warp working left to right. Move wire wraps and cut material to keep splices on the bottom of the seat.

Wonky Single Strand: Spritz the top and the bottom of the offending area. Look for the closest wire wrap and remove the splice. Adjust tension as necessary and replace the wire wrap.

WEAVING THE WEFT

For this project, we are weaving the top and bottom of the seat in a 3-under/3-over twill.

More compact (2x2) twill patterns and plain weave patterns are VERY difficult to weave. Complicated patterns such as diamonds, chevrons, etc., combine twill weaves stepping forward and backward. Refer to Pattern Mapping and Example Patterns Appendix for inspiration.

The hardest part for new weavers is figuring out where to start at the sides. The pattern takes time to learn. Our students seem to "get it" after weaving a third of the way down the side rails. Refer often to The Twill Pattern skill box for guidance. Wet the warp before you start and periodically as you weave for best results.

12 underside of chair at back

13 top of chair at back

11 Plan before you weave. Start with the chair upside down. The end of the first weaver strand should tuck under the last three warp strands on the left at the back rail. To make this happen, use three fingers to count the furthest left three warps as "under," then move to the right and count the next three warps as "over," then 3-under/3-over, etc. You may end up with one or two warp strands at the opposite side. That is fine.

12 Weave Row 1 on the bottom. Grab a medium/long strand of reed. Check for top and bottom. Start at the right, weave the way you determined so the end is tucked under the last three warps on the left. Push the end of the reed close to the back rail to secure it. The pattern on the bottom of the seat will slant slightly.

13 Weave Row 1 on the top. Flip the chair upright. Start going over three warp strands at the right rear post. Then 3-under/3-over, and repeat to the end of the row. Pull the strand tight against the side rail without pulling the weave out of the bottom. Push Row 1 back toward the back rail.

WEAVING THE WEFT (CONTINUED)

14 Weave Row 2 on the bottom. This is where the twill pattern begins to take shape. Think of it as a stair step. The end of the strand went under three last time. Now, step back one warp strand and go under two. Continue across with 3-over/3-under. Pull strand taut against the rail and push Row 2 tightly against Row 1.

15 Weave Row 2 on the top. Flip the chair right-side up. Row 2 you will go over 2 strands, then continue 3-over/3-under across the row. Pull the strand tight against the rail and push Row 2 up against Row 1.

16 Continue weaving top and bottom until you run out of reed (typically 2-3 rows per strand). If you come to a V-splice, treat it as one strand if it overlaps at all. If the V strands are parallel to each other treat them as separate strands. Splice on a new strand.

17 Continue weaving top and bottom, splicing strands when necessary and using an occasional medium length strand. As you get comfortable with the pattern, start practicing using a tool and compress weaver strands that are bowing.

18 You may break a sweat weaving the last few rows! Keep making space by adjusting rows back. Use your ramp tool. You might even need to weave half the row, pull the reed, then weave the rest of the row.

SKILL // USING A RAMP

At first it is easy to push weaver strands through the warps. A tool will be necessary as the weave gets tighter and especially when filling in the gussets.

SKILL // THE TWILL PATTERN

A stairstep pattern achieved when each new weaver row steps back by one warp strand.

SKILL // SPLICING WEAVER STRANDS

When splicing weft/weaver strands, simply overlap the old strand with the new strand. The tension within the pattern holds the splice in place.

1. Clip the old strand so that it ends over the warp strands.
2. Wet the new strand and find top/bottom.
3. Weave backward following the same pattern as the old strand.
4. Slide the new strand on top of the old strand. Hide the end of the new strand under the warp strands.

Splicing Rules:

- Splice on the bottom of a seat or the back of a back.
- Splice overlap should be ~8".

WEAVING THE WEFT (CONTINUED)

SKILL // COMPRESSING THE PATTERN

The weaver rows may start to bow toward the front rail. Use a hammer and screwdriver to tap material back to make space. Start with Row 1 on the top of the seat. Then tap material back on the bottom. Tap back reed along the side rails. Be careful not to chip the reed.

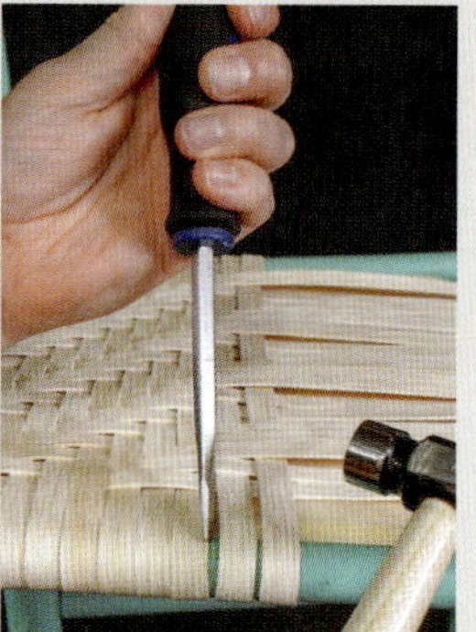

SKILL // INCHWORM TECHNIQUE

The Inchworm Technique gives you a little more leverage to maneuver the weaver strand through the tight seat. Make an 8" loop to push the weaver over/under a few warp strands. Pull the slack out a little, then repeat. [Refer to Materials, Tools & Skills Library]

19 Finish weaving on the bottom. Continue the pattern as far as you can. Clip excess reed close to the corner post. For trapezoidal seats, the end will be covered by the gusset strands. For rectangular projects, tuck the end under three (or more) warp strands. It's OK if the pattern isn't perfect on the bottom.

If you are weaving a rectangular footstool or barstool, you are done weaving! Skip the gusset fill-ins and go directly to Cleaning Up and Sealing the Seat.

TRAPEZOIDAL SEATS—FILLING THE GUSSETS

Most chairs require 2-3 fill-in strands on each side, but every chair is different. If the chair is old and quirky, it may need three on the left and one on the right. We've waited until the end for this project, but intermediate weavers or ambitious beginners can start adding fill-ins strands when the side rails are half full (that's what we do).

PRO TIP: *Pattern Guide*

New weavers often get confused with the pattern whenever they turn the chair around. Use a short piece of reed to simulate the "3-over" weaver strand. Track a diagonal line of "3-overs" near the center of the pattern and move it "downstairs" toward the row you have to weave, then count back to determine how to start.

21

20 Prepare to weave. Spray the gusset weaver strands. Spin the chair so the left side is facing you. Notice the pattern is the same as it was when you were looking at the front: 3-over/3-under. You'll start at the inside and move toward the side rail.

21 Weave the first fill-in strand into the top of the seat. Grab a short strand, soak it, and find the top side! Weave toward the back following the pattern. Tuck the end near the back post. Bring the long end under the seat for now.

WEAVING THE WEFT (CONTINUED)

SKILL // TENSIONING TIGHT SPOTS

Grab the strand solidly with needle-nose pliers without doing damage. Tap the side of the pliers to give yourself a little extra oomph in those areas that are impossible to get into by hand.

22 Keep adding fill-in strands until the left front rail is full. Tuck the end into the pattern at the side rail, but don't try to weave on top of the side rail. Compress the warp strands toward the middle of the chair to make space when necessary. Tuck the long ends under the front rail for now.

23 Add fill-ins to the right gusset. Spin the chair so that the right rail is facing you. Weave fill-in strands on the right side until the front rail is completely full.

24 Weave fill-ins into the bottom. Turn the chair upside down and weave loose strands into the bottom starting in the middle of the seat and moving out. At the V-splices, it will be tricky. It's OK to deviate from the pattern slightly on the bottom or run strands on top of each other.

23

24

CLEANING UP AND SEALING THE SEAT

25a

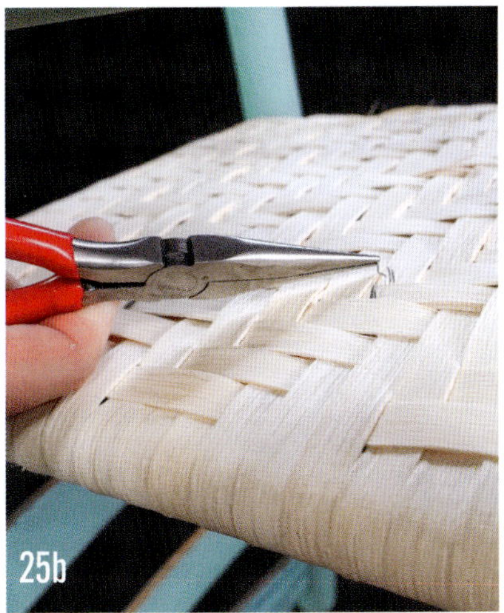
25b

25c

25d

26a

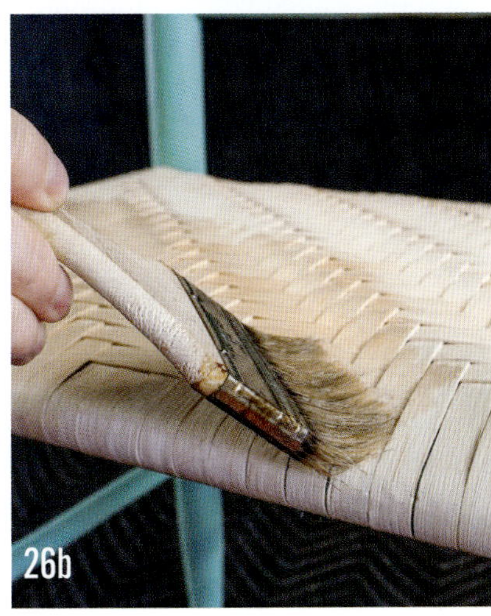
26b

25 Remove visible wire wraps by working an awl under the wrap, clipping the wire and removing it with needle nose pliers **[25a & 25b]**. Clip ends that are longer than ¼" **[25c]**. Clip fibers sticking up with small scissors **[25d]**. Don't pull on the fibers or you risk damaging the reed.

PRO TIP: *Trimmers*

Save your hands and use a tool.

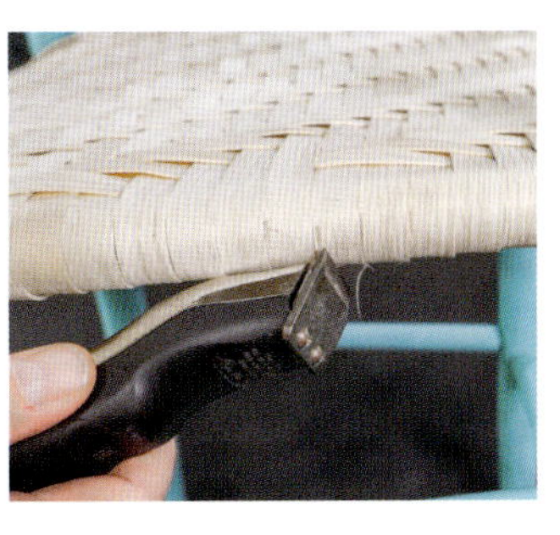

26 Let the chair dry overnight before sealing the seat. Start with the chair upside down and brush the finish on the bottom of the seat. Turn the chair right-side up and clean up any drips along the edges of the seat with your brush. Brush the finish on the top of the seat. [Refer to Materials, Tools & Skills Library]

27 Sit back and enjoy! Give yourself a high-five or do a little dance.

There is more than one way to weave a chair. Some people prefer to start weaving at the front. Some people put fill-ins in partially through the weaving process. Weaving is full of personal choices and different methods work better for different people.

MAINTENANCE

Splint reed chairs are best kept indoors, away from heat sources and out of direct sunlight. Seats can be vacuumed to remove detritus and spot-cleaned with a mild soap solution. Apply additional coats of your preferred sealant as needed.

OLD HICKORY FURNITURE

The designs of these classic chairs and rockers present a few uniquechallenges including large, curvedbacks, central-back support rails and tight, tapered joints. Before weaving, wrap tapered joints to reduce breakage along the length when using splint reed.

DESIGN TIPS

Avoid rails with a rectangular profile—the sharp edges will break the reed.

Avoid curved rails—the reed will not lay flat and is prone to breakage.

Avoid slots—material will shred when threading through small openings.

BINDER CANE

MATERIAL

Binder cane is cut from the outer edge of the rattan palm. It is a larger (4-10mm) version of the cane strands used in laced/hand caning. Slab rattan (8-10mm) is notorious for slicing your hands, so be careful!

PREPARATION

Soak coils in warm water for 10-15 minutes until it is flexible and no longer feels/sounds crunchy.

PROCESS

Keeping enough slack in the warp can be tricky because it shrinks when it dries. Wrap the warp around a dowel to keep the tension of the extra slack uniform.

The twill pattern is the same but you can vary the number of warps over/under, anywhere from 2-over/2-under up to 7-over/7-under twills. The smaller the ratio or the smaller the material, the more tedious and time-consuming the process will be. The rounded top of the binder cane makes packing tight patterns more challenging.

Chair woven by Mitch Palminteri of Friend of Furniture.

KENNEDY ROCKER/ PORCH WEAVE

The Kennedy rocker is traditionally woven in binder cane with a twill seat and a "porch weave" back. These chairs are physically demanding and tedious weaving projects. Honestly, we've priced ourselves out of handweaving these projects over the years.

PRO TIP:

Buy Replacement Parts

At the time of this writing, replacement seats and backs for Kennedy rockers can be purchased directly from the manufacturer: www.KennedyRockers.com

INTRODUCTION TO HICKORY BARK

Harvesting photos courtesy of Andy Glenn

Natural bark stripped from hickory trees creates a beautiful, strong seat. The harvesting is so labor intensive that most people who do the work (rightly) reserve it for their own chairs. Ideally the tree is harvested in late spring or early summer when sap is running and the bark is slipping. Once a tree is felled, both the rough outer bark and the inner bark, or bast, are removed and the inner bark is then coiled and dried for storage. A smaller 8 inch diameter tree can produce one round of bark while larger 12"-14" diameters, you may be able to squeeze two rounds from the bast. Bark is typically almost as tall as the tree, 25'-40' lengths. As it is a natural product, inclusions and mineral deposits may occur throughout. Knots certainly occur regularly and, in my experience, they usually show up at the front rail requiring me to cut the length ... grr. At the time of writing, other hand-split wooden splints like oak and ash are hard to come by for chair seating purposes. (Foxfire Books have documented this process and it is worth a look.) Current commercially available split ash feels a little too thin for weight-bearing seats and are generally intended for backs and basketry.

Notable bark chairmakers/weavers with fascinating histories worth researching are Richard Poyner of central Tennessee (a former enslaved person who bought his freedom before the Civil War) and 20th-century chairmaker/weaver Chester Cornett of Kentucky (the Salvador Dali of post and rung construction). Old Hickory Furniture chairs with bark seats date back to the late 1800s, and are still highly collectible and stylish despite having a similar design as they did 100 years ago. Contemporary hickory bark chairs became increasingly elegant and refined as seen on side chairs and rocking chairs by Brian Boggs (Berea, Ky./Asheville, N.C.) who influenced a new generation of contemporary chairmakers. More traditional and highly desirable chairs by Lyle Wheeler of North Wilkesboro, N.C., and Terry Ratliff of Floyd County Kentucky give a nod to historical chair design. Eric Cannizzaro of Vermont and Andy Glenn of Maine are innovative Chair Nerds whose diversity in material, finishes, and construction are astonishing. Jeff Lefkowitz in Virginia and David Douyard in Connecticut have helped hundreds of chairmakers learn to build chairs and weave with bark. Jeff's technical manuals are an art form in and of themselves.

Hickory Bark strips are soaked, shaved thin, and cut into "even" strips before weaving. They are leathery in feel and bacon-y in appearance. The first "warp" strand is tied around the back rail then wrapped around the span of front and back rails. We prefer to taper the warp strands so they are wider at the front rail eliminating "fillers" at the gusset. To save precious material, transition warp-to-weft with a wrap around the back post. The "weft" or "weaver" strands are commonly woven in a 3-over/3-under twill pattern. Splints are spliced together on the bottom of the seat. Once dried, the seat is lightly sanded and finished with oil. Bark shrinks and tightens when it dries producing a firm, solid seat that lasts for decades.

Photo courtesy of Brian Boggs Chairmakers

Six-slat Grand Rocker by Lyle Wheeler

Photo courtesy of David Douyard

AFTER ALL IS SAID AND DONE

PAPER RUSH PROJECT

// TIME: ~3-8 HOURS //

Paper rush (aka fiber rush or fibre rush) is a single-ply, twisted kraft paper cord commonly produced in sizes ranging from $\frac{4}{32}$" to $\frac{6}{32}$". Although commonly available in varying shades of brown, paper rush can be found in vibrant colors or you can dye your own. Color accents are a way to add complexity to a plain brown seat.

Paper rush originated in the early 20th century after an embargo limited rattan imports. American Marshall Lloyd developed a more durable, less expensive way of producing wicker furniture, substituting paper cord for round rattan reed. Chairmakers and manufacturers quickly realized the potential for replacing twisted grasses with paper rush.

Paper rush is woven in a figure-eight pattern across opposing rails, with a 90° turn forming the tight corners. Weaving starts at the posts and moves in toward the center. Because most chairs are wider in the front than the back, the front corners (or gussets) must be filled in with short strands. The finished pattern forms a series of adjoining triangles connected by a horizontal bridge in the middle. The triangular sections are stuffed with cardboard to add structural support. A balance of tension and consistent adjustments are necessary throughout the process.

Refer to Materials, Tools & Skills Library for more detailed information.

**** Denotes tools that are helpful, but optional.***

TOOLS

Spring Clamps

Hammer

Flathead Screwdriver

Snips or Scissors

Needle-nose Pliers

Utility Knife/Blade

Measuring Tape/Ruler/Pencil

Water Tub/Bucket

Towel(s)/Washcloth

Paintbrush

Spritz Bottle*

MATERIALS

Steel Tacks

2-2.5 lb Paper Rush

Cardboard

Glue

Masking Tape*

Protective Coating (Shellac, Polyurethane, etc.)

BASIC SKILLS

Marking Gussets

Tacking

Clamping

Compressing on the Rails

Apply Protective Coating

Paper Rush: The size of the chair seat determines how much material you will need. Paper rush is measured in weight and not length. Generally, you need 2-2.5 lb of material for an "average" seat (approx. 17" between the front posts). Consult your supplier for help. It's always better to order more material than you think you'll need as colors can vary slightly. Deciding what size material to use is a balance between workability, project scale, and weaving time. Larger material (6⁄32" or 7⁄32") is harder to manipulate, but it takes less time to finish a project. Smaller material (4⁄32" or 5⁄32") is easier to work with, but it takes longer to weave. We primarily use a 5⁄32" material which is a good middle-path option.

Cardboard: Use standard-thickness cardboard with at least one kraft-brown side. Colored cardboard may peek through the cords and be visible on the new seat. Extra-thick, heavy duty cardboard is impossible to manipulate. Thin, light-duty boxes don't provide very much support and it takes a lot to properly stuff the seat. A local frame shop is a perfect place to get large glass and mat board boxes. Or try a local cardboard recycling center.

Chair Frame: Most post and rung chairs have straight, round rails. Older, handmade versions often have hand-sculpted "aerofoil" rails.

Certain structural elements complicate the project: Skirts, arms, spindles and floating seats are a few. [For Hitchcock and Windsor chairs, refer to Special Cases—Disassembly Required.]

Arm supports that pass through the rail require weaving through a small slot and adding extra wraps on the rail.

Rush slides on concave and convex rails.

Score curved rails to keep material from shifting.

PRO TIP: ***Removable Seats***

According to chairmakers, removable seats are easier to weave. As weavers, we find that they are more difficult due to the lack of a frame to pull against. Seats with wrapped corners are even more tedious and varied. We couldn't possibly include all the various wraps manufactures have come up with. It's a reverse engineering process, so take photos, take notes, and do your best! No matter the style, use bar clamps to support the seat and simulate a chair frame.

BEFORE YOU WEAVE

Take a before photo of the chair! It's fun to see before and after. You may not want to use the previous seat as a guide—the previous weaver could have made mistakes.

Remove the old seat. Use a blade, snips, or scissors. If using a blade, cut along the inside of the rails; cutting on the rails can damage them. A sawing motion usually works best. Cut from the posts to the middle, rotating the chair around. This helps avoid accidentally cutting the post. Peel the material off of the rails and push the old material down. Remove any tacks/staples in the rails. If you can't remove them, hammer them flush.

Address structural issues. [Refer to Structural Issues & Repairs]

Prepare the chair frame. Wipe down the frame. We like Howard Feed-N-Wax or tung oil to nourish the wood. Leave the seat rails raw. Wax and oil make them slippery.

Calculate and mark gussets. [Refer to Materials, Tools & Skills Library] Most chairs are trapezoidal and have gussets. For rectangular projects, there are no gussets. Skip the marking, but pay attention to the material handling and pattern instructions in that section. Your step-by-step weaving instructions start at Step 12.

PRO TIP: ***The "Deep-Seated" Exception***

The standard 1:1 rush weave shouldn't be used on "deep-seated" chair frames. Compare the lengths of the side rail and the back rail. If the side rail is longer, refer to the "Continental Weave" section later in this chapter. You will learn how to deal with deep seats while maintaining comfort and structural integrity.

SKILL // MATERIAL WRANGLING

Paper rush is a twisted material that will try to work its way into a wonderfully annoying rat's nest if left to its own devices.

Coiling the material is the best way to tame it. When making a coil, pay close attention to the material's natural twist. You may have to untwist or retwist the material to keep it looping nicely. Forcing the material onto a shuttle or wrapping it around your forearm can cause kinks or open up the twist, causing weak points. Keep your material happy and it will make weaving easier.

Instead of setting the coil down on the work surface to unravel, hang it on the back post or on a clamp. When you have to set the coil down on the work surface, put a tool on top of it or clamp around the coil so that it doesn't "slinky" all over the place.

FILLING THE GUSSETS

1 Carefully coil the material into a ~10" loop of material that fits comfortably in the palm of your hand. You can make several coils at once or as needed.

2 Wet one of the small coils. Dry paper rush is stiff and becomes more pliable when wet. Submerge a coil for a couple of seconds, but don't soak it. The twisted paper becomes unusable when it gets too wet as it untwists, overtwists, and pills. Once you take the material out of the tub, work the water into the coil by crunching the coil together and moving the material around. Smack the material onto a towel to remove any extra water. Alternatively, you can spritz the coil until it is pliable.

3 Tack the end of the coil to the left side rail. Drive the tack into the *side* of the rail and not the top. The tack should be approximately ½" from the end of the strand and 1" from the front post. Make sure the tack is fully seated and flush with the material.

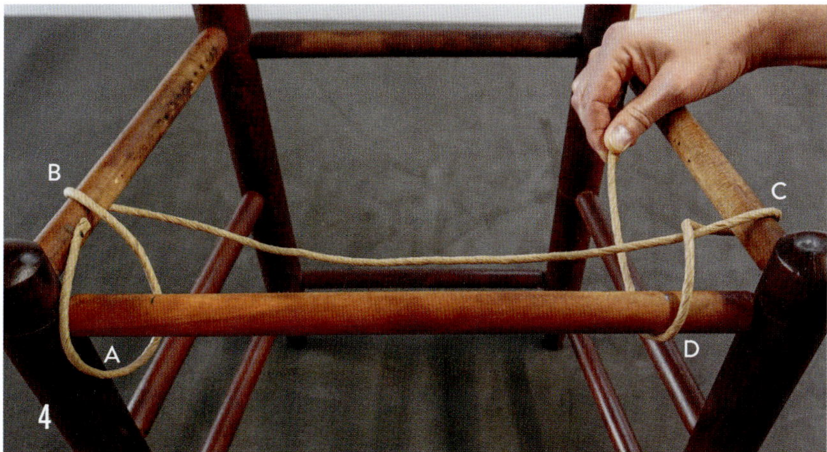

4 **[A]** Loosely wrap the coil over the front rail and up the middle of the seat frame (straightaway). **[B]** Then wrap the coil over the left rail and up the middle again (corner). The first post is loosely wrapped. **[C]** Bring the coil over the right rail and up the middle of the seat (straightaway). **[D]** Then wrap the coil over the front rail and up the middle (corner). Hang the coil on the back post. Two posts ... loosely wrapped!

PRO TIP:
Pneumatic Stapler

To save time and effort, use a pneumatic stapler instead of tacks. We use an upholstery stapler that shoots a 23 gauge, 3/16" crown staple in varying leg lengths.

5 Tension around both front posts. Apply maximum tension on the straightaway. Intentionally change directions with a crisp corner and pull just enough tension to hold the corner tight. Clamp on the rail to hold the tension.

Rush Pattern Mantra

"Over the Rail > Up the Middle
[Turn the Corner]
Over the Rail > Up the Middle"

If you are ever bringing the material down the middle, something in the pattern is incorrect. If the pattern looks wrong, it likely is. Repeat the mantra.

Tao of Chair

Focus on one action at a time.

Wrap the pattern loosely and focus on the pattern.

Tension the loose strands and focus on the tension.

SKILL // TACKING—HAVING TROUBLE?

Refer to Materials, Tools & Skills Library on pages 20-26.

FILLING THE GUSSETS (CONTINUED)

SKILL // TENSIONING

The rush pattern consists of a series of "straightaways" and "corners." It's important to keep tension throughout the process, but not always maximum tension. Pulling maximum tension on the "corner" will bring the pattern out of 90°. Make an intentional corner every time.

Pull maximum tension on the "straightaway."

Keep tension by pinching the strand around the rail. Don't fight friction and try to pull more tension when the strand is already wrapped around the rail.

Hold the tension on the rail with one hand while transferring the tension to the working strand that goes up the middle of the seat.

Make an intentional corner that pulls the two straightaway strands together and doesn't crowd previous strands. It's helpful if you pull the initial straightaway down slightly.

6 Adjust the "corner" juncture to sit between the rails. Pay special attention to corners where the initial straightaway strand wraps over the higher rail.

7 Tack the loose end on the inside of the right side rail (not on top) and clip strand. With the clamp on the front rail, tack the working end a few inches back from the post. Cut the rush ~½" from the tack.

8 Add two more gusset strands sequentially (three total). Tack the left rail and loosely wrap the coil around both front corners. Tension the pattern and then tack the end of the strand on the right rail. Each tack should be approximately ¾" further up the rail from the last tack.

9 Make adjustments on both of the front corners. Small adjustments make all the difference between a clean, uniform seat and one that is lumpy and uneven. It's best to make adjustments every three wraps as the pattern progresses. Put a sticky note on your chair if you need a reminder. Adjusting every three strands is very important!

FILLING THE GUSSETS (CONTINUED)

SKILL // PATTERN ADJUSTMENTS

The goals when adjusting are to get the maximum amount of material on the rails and to ensure that the corners of the pattern stay at 90°.

Three is the magic number. Adjust every three strands. Adjusting more often slows down the process and the adjustments don't stay in place. Adjusting less often results in extra slack and a lumpy seat. As you get comfortable weaving rush, you may try adjusting every 4-6 strands ... but you'll never go wrong adjusting every three strands. Do the best you can and move on. Over-adjusting is a real thing and repeated effort in one area can hurt more than it helps.

Use the flat side of a flathead screwdriver as a paddle. Tap the shaft of the screwdriver with a hammer. You can apply more force, and you're less likely to hit the chair frame.

Adjustment 1

Compress material on the rails, working toward each post. Avoid compressing if you are working the pattern way out of 90° or working on a convex curve.

Before compression.

After compression.

Compress on both rails in every corner.

Material bunched up; corner not 90°.

Adjustment 2

Rework "corners" of the pattern to 90°. The first few strands will hug the round posts. Work them to 90° over 4-5 strands and not all at once. Compress or expand the pattern as necessary. Small gaps between strands are acceptable and uniform gaps are preferable to corners out of 90°. Recompress on the rail when necessary.

Remove material overlap; shift corner closer to 90°.

Compress in the corner slightly.

Remove extra space adjusting created.

Uniform corner at 90°.

Make the same adjustments on the bottom. The "bottom" of the seat is never going to look quite as clean as the top, but it shouldn't be neglected. Any big issues (overlaps, kinks, etc.) on the bottom can affect the top.

FILLING THE GUSSETS (CONTINUED)

10

10 Keep adding strands until you reach your gusset mark. Adjust every three strands as they're added. When you think you are at your gusset mark, make a final adjustment on the rails.

11 Verify gusset measurement. Double check your gusset by measuring the distance between the rush strands on the front rail and comparing it to the distance between the back posts. If you are within one strand width, continue to the next step. If the two measurements are not within a strand width, add or remove strands accordingly before proceeding.

PRO TIP: *Gauging and adjusting distance between tacks*

When the strands approach the halfway point to the gusset mark, the tacks should be approximately halfway up the rail. Expand or contract the distance between the tacks accordingly so that the last gusset tack is close to the back post. Due to rail height differences, the tacks on the right side naturally progress up the rail quicker and tacking distances should be slightly smaller.

WRAPPING THE SEAT

Tao of Chair: Get Moving

Rotating your chair while tensioning helps you get more leverage and avoid injury. It can be difficult to pull away from yourself when tensioning the back corners.

PRO TIP: *Spritzing*

When adjusting, sometimes the strands won't stay put. Try giving the strands or the rail a light spritz. Use this type of spritzing sparingly or the material can pill and look funny.

12 Wrap all four posts loosely. Start with a tack on the left rail close to the back post. Loosely wrap the front posts and instead of stopping at the front right post, continue the pattern to include the back posts. The pattern never changes, you are always "over-the-rail" and "up-the-middle".

13 Tension the pattern. Work your way from the tack using "straightaway" and "corner" tensioning methods. Use a clamp on the rail to hold the tension.

14 Continue to wrap corners and tension the pattern until you run out of coiled material. *Adjust every three strands!*

WRAPPING THE SEAT (CONTINUED)

15 Splice in a new coil. Don't forget to wet it.

16 Continue to wrap corners, tension the pattern, and splice in new coils until the side rails are approximately halfway full of rush. Don't forget to adjust every three strands on the top and bottom of the seat!

17 Fill gaps in pattern with cardboard. For stability, comfort and longevity, the gap in between the middle/top layers of the rush pattern should be filled. An added bonus is that adding cardboard evens out the pattern nicely.

Tao of Chair: Know Yourself

Give yourself a break. Weave as much or as little as you're comfortable with. Don't risk shoulder/wrist/elbow injuries by pushing your limits. The end of a coil is a perfect time to take a break.

Clamp on the empty part of the rail when you take a break. The rush you've already woven will dent when clamped for an extended period of time. If you forget and get a dent on your pattern, spritz/wet the area and fluff it back up by tapping it with a hammer.

SKILL // SPLICING ON A NEW STRAND

You can splice along any of the four "straightaways." As the pattern progresses, the top and bottom layers of rush cover up the middle layer and hide the knots. A square knot is preferable and sits cleanly within the pattern. It looks like two intersecting "U"s with the strands lining up next to each other. Make sure both strands are good and wet for pliability. Keep knots at least 1" away from corners of the pattern. You can adjust the location of the knot easily by opening it up and moving the "U"s side-to-side. When you are happy with the location, pull the knot tight and give it a squish with pliers.

Eventually, you'll have to splice on the bottom of the seat where it will be seen. Locate the knot closer to the middle of the seat than the rail, but not so close to the middle that it interferes with the weaving.

STUFFING THE SEAT

There are four quadrants with gaps to fill once the pattern is at the halfway point. If you try to fit cardboard too early in the process, it moves around and gets in your way. If you wait too long, it's difficult to work the cardboard into the gaps.

In most chairs, the front and back sections are isosceles triangles. The side sections are mirrored, scalene triangles with the longer leg reaching toward the front of the seat. The quadrants might not require the same number of cardboard triangles depending on the pattern tension and rail shape.

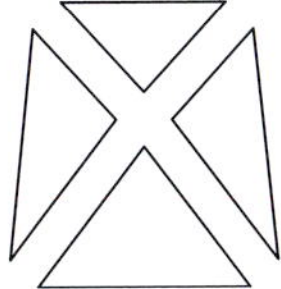

We use a series of cardboard triangles, but we've seen all kinds of materials inside of rush seats: envelopes, cloth, cereal boxes, and newspapers: time capsules from decades past. Older chairs often have stacks of veneer or bunched up plant fibers as stuffing.

CUT & FIT A TEMPLATE

Cut a triangle of cardboard that is approximately 1" smaller than the section you are stuffing. You can take measurements or estimate by holding a piece of cardboard on top of the pattern.

Slide one corner fully into the pattern. Bend cardboard in the middle and slide the other corner into the pattern.

If the piece fits snug and doesn't crumple, remove it and use it as a template. Most seats need 3-4 pieces per quadrant.

STAGGER THE CARDBOARD

The goal is to fully fill the quadrants without adding bulk in the center. The gap is wider at the rails and slopes down to nothing in the center of the pattern, so stairstepping the cardboard is necessary.

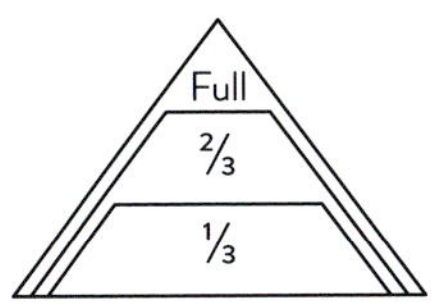

PRO TIP: *Cutting Triangles*

Cut cardboard triangles with a little help from the Pythagorean Theorem: $A^2 + B^2 = C^2$

This method works best for the front and back quadrants with two sides the same length [A=B].

Determine C by subtracting 2" from the distance between the posts. (Typical chair is ~17" between the posts, making C=15.) Calculate A with the following equation.

$$A=\sqrt{\frac{C^2}{2}}$$

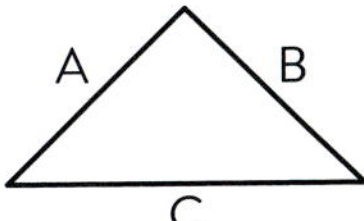

Example with C=15

$$A=\sqrt{\frac{15^2}{2}} \quad A=\sqrt{\frac{225}{2}} \quad A=\sqrt{112.5} \quad A=10.60 \text{ or } \approx 10\tfrac{3}{4}$$

Cut a square of cardboard with A-length edges. Then cut the square on the diagonal and you have two triangles ready to go!

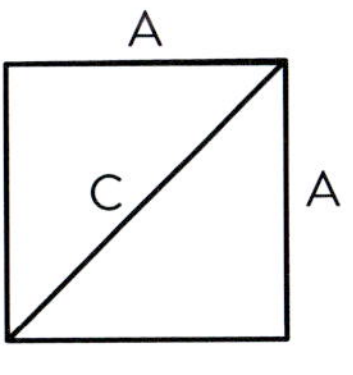

PRO TIP: *Working with Corrugation*

Bending a triangle of cardboard is very difficult if you are fighting corrugation running side-to-side. The cardboard crumples when pushed into the pattern when the corrugation runs top-to-bottom. When the corrugation runs diagonally, you get a combination of strength and flexibility. Minimize waste and maximize the attributes of the cardboard by cutting squares/rectangles first and then cut them diagonally.

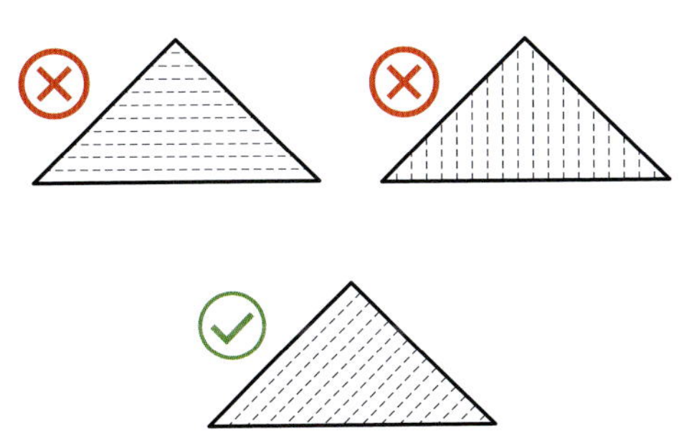

STUFFING THE SEAT (CONTINUED)

19a

19b

18 Slide a full triangle into the pattern close to the rail and pull it toward the center.

19 Slide partial triangles (trapezoids) next to the rail until there is only space for one more triangle.

20 Slide the final/full triangle into place next to the rail. *Two full triangles should sandwich the partial triangles.*

PRO TIP: *Dealing with Cardboard*

The left and right quadrants are mirrors of each other. The template for one side fits upside down in the other.

Colors on the cardboard are OK, but must face down or they can show through the cords on the seat.

Use a screwdriver to make space before fitting the next piece of cardboard.

Use a screwdriver to push the last piece of cardboard into place.

Rectangular rails: For extra protection against breakage, add another triangular piece of cardboard on top the rail, covering the sharp edge.

WRAPPING THE SEAT (CONTINUED)

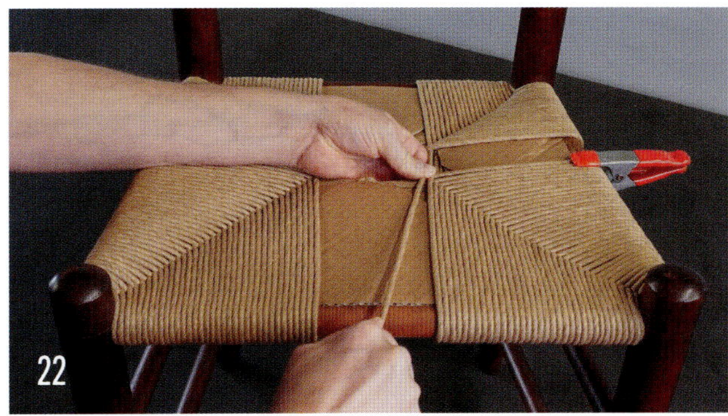

SKILL // NAVIGATING TIGHT SPACES

As the hole in the center of the pattern shrinks, your working coils must shrink as well. The best coil is just small enough to fit through the hole without much effort. Instead of reaching your hand through the hole, try using two hands to push the coil from below.

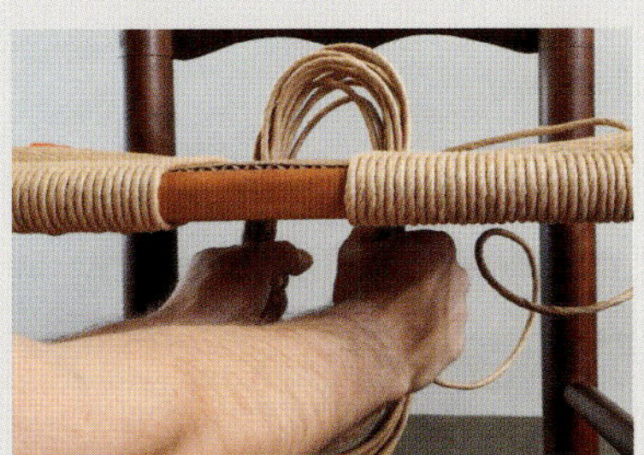

When the center hole is too small to fit a coil, you have to pull one strand at a time. To prevent excessive twisting, pull a "loop" through instead of starting with the end of the strand. Keep one hand underneath the chair to help manage material twists. A twist that goes unnoticed is a mistake that adds slack into the weave and must be remedied. Unweave to the offending area, untwist and reweave.

21 In order to pass the working coil up through the middle of the seat, you'll need to make some space. Remove the tips of the cardboard triangles, leaving a playing-card sized hole. Be careful and use a sawing motion with a blade/utility knife. It's easy to slip and cut yourself or strands you've already woven and tensioned. Been there, done that!

22 Continue to weave the pattern loosely and then tension. Don't forget to adjust every three strands. The middle layer of rush always stays below the cardboard filler.

Pay attention to the pattern as it approaches the center. It's difficult to determine which small opening is truly the "middle."

23 Fill up the side rails. Follow the pattern until the very end. Make space for tensioning strands by adjusting more often.

WRAPPING THE SEAT (CONTINUED)

SKILL // WHEN IS ENOUGH, ENOUGH?

When you think the rail is full, check if there is space for another strand. Put a flathead screwdriver into the top of the pattern and turn it sideways. (1) Strands move out of the way easily: Not enough. You can fit at least one more strand. (2) Strands buckle and jump on top of each other: That's enough. See completed photo below.

Note: The bottom of the seat usually fills quicker than the top. It's OK if the last few bottom strands don't lay flat.

Looks good, but check for space.

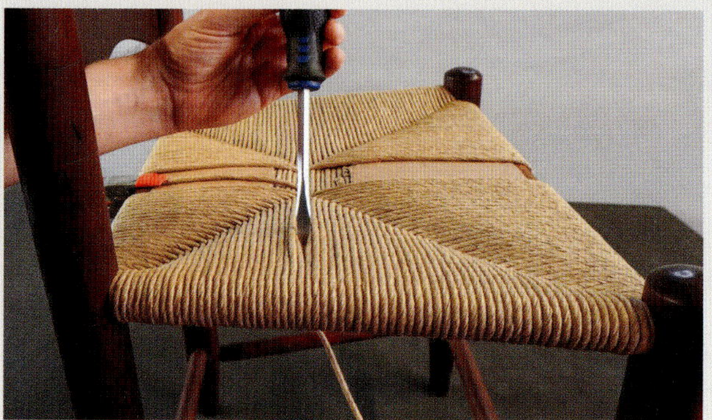

That's enough!

If you need to squeeze in another strand, start with standard compression on the rail.

Use a flathead screwdriver on the rail and turn it sideways to coax stubborn strands.

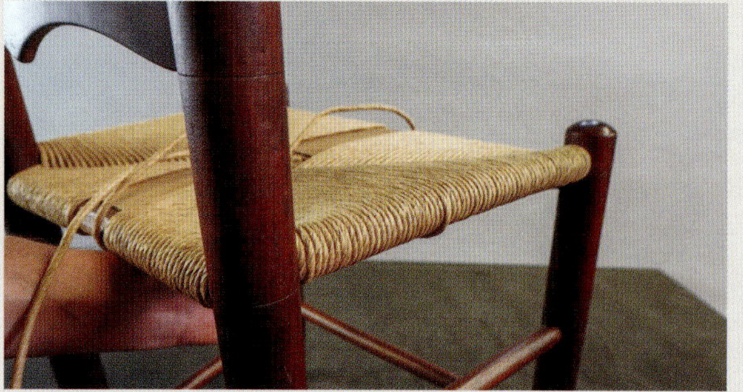

Avoid a bulging strand by focusing space-making efforts on the bottom of the rail. Pulling the working strand toward the middle of the seat and very tight against the rail can slide the other strands out of the way.

THE BRIDGE

PRO TIP: *Adjust for parallel lines instead of 90°*

As the material on the rails gets closer together, it can be tricky to visualize 90°. It's easier to ensure that each quadrant's paired strands are parallel to each other. Measure the distance at the center of the pattern (A) and at edge (B). The measurements need to be within a strand width for the pattern to meet cleanly in the center.

Each quadrant is measured and adjusted separately. The front/back or side/side measurements may or may not be the same.

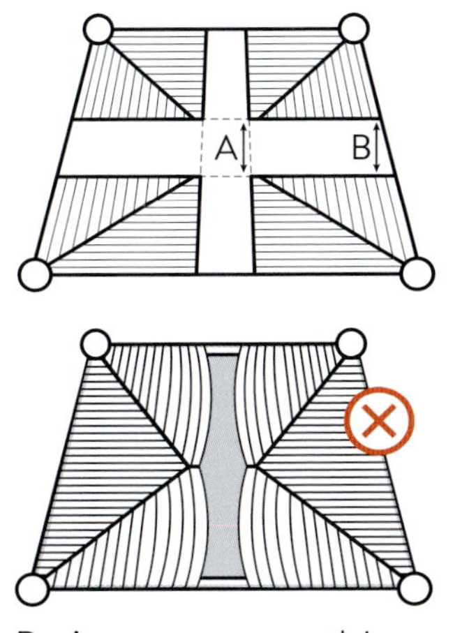

Don't compress too much in the center and edge, leaving an hourglass shape.

24 Begin the bridge by wrapping the rush around the front and back rails only. Start wrapping on whichever side of the gap the working strand ended and work toward the opposite side. Follow the pattern to decide whether to wrap toward the front rail or the back rail first. If you are uncertain, measure the empty space on the front and back rails and wrap toward the larger space.

25 Wrap three strands loosely, then tension them. The mantra doesn't change, it's still "over the rail and up the middle." Make compression adjustments on the rails and in the middle. Splice on more material as necessary.

PRO TIP: *Avoid Another Splice*

Estimate the amount of material to finish the bridge. When you think you're ready for the last bundle of material, measure the area you have left on the rail and count how many strands it would take to fill that area. Most chairs, front-to-back, are about the size of your forearm. Wrap the material around your forearm as many times as you count and don't forget to add one wrap so you don't run short.

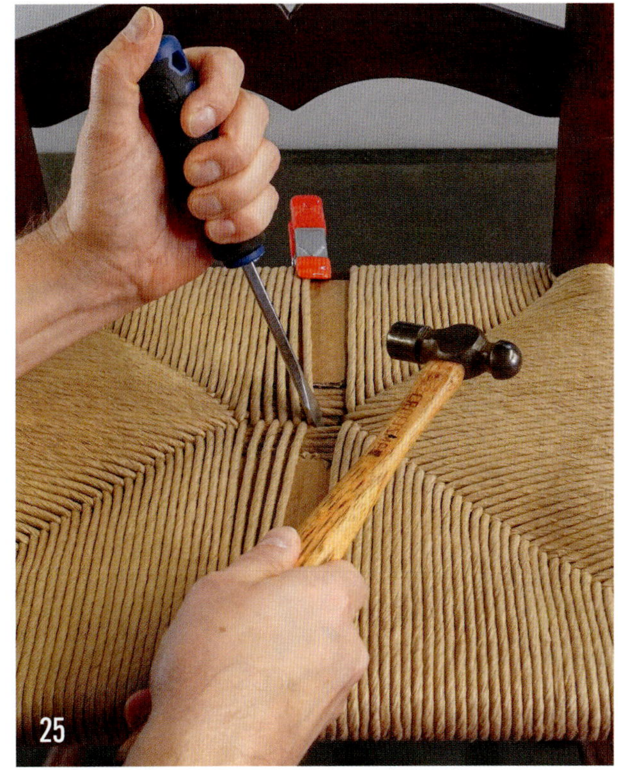

THE BRIDGE (CONTINUED)

SKILL // THREADING THE NEEDLE

To make sure you get enough material on the rails, you have to become a space-making expert. The hole you are threading through becomes almost nonexistent. The following techniques can be used separately or in conjunction with each other.

- Wrap the end of the working strand with masking tape.
- Use needle-nose pliers pushed through the hole from the bottom of the seat. Pushing down from the top can cause visible harm to the material.
- Use the working strand to open up space by pulling it away from the pattern.

26 Finish the bridge by adding material until the front and back rails are completely full.

THE FINAL KNOT

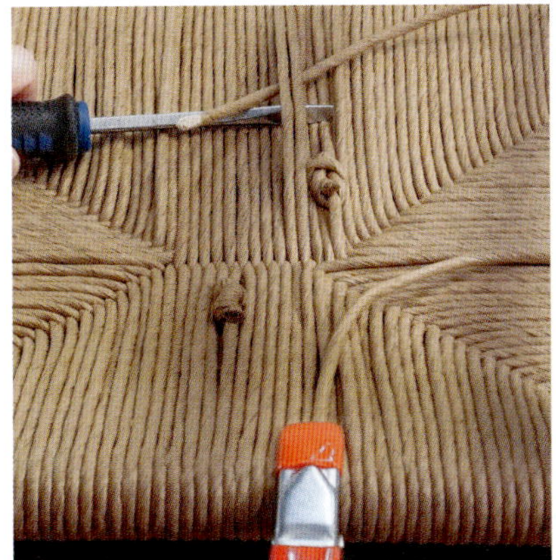
Use a tool to make space under two strands opposite your working strand and thread the working strand under them.

Pull tension on the working strand and swing the working strand around to lock the tension in place.

Use a tool to make space and thread the working strand under itself and a neighboring strand.

Pull the circle you just made taut.

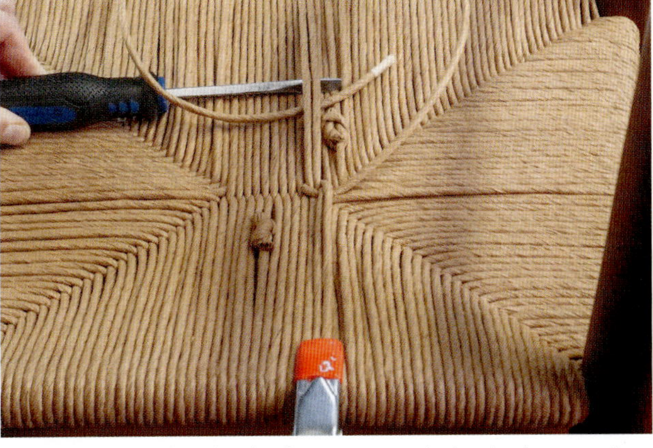
Thread the strand under the first two strands, but in the opposite direction, creating a loop.

Thread the strand through the loop created

Pull the knot tight and clip the end.

FINISHING THE SEAT (CONTINUED)

27 Add glue to visible knots. The knots are not likely to back out, but it could happen if they get a little help from a feline friend or small fingers. This step ensures that the knots will stay in place no matter what.

28 Adjust strands for uniform spacing. Shuffle strands on the rail and adjust corners. On the side rails, start by working toward the front, then go toward the back.

29 Burnish lumpy areas of the seat. Spritz the area lightly and then rub it with the wooden part of a hammer or the side of a screwdriver.

27

29a

29b

30

30 Apply a protective finish, but let the seat dry overnight first. [Refer to Materials, Tools & Skills Library]

31 Give yourself a high-five and a treat for successfully completing your project!

MAINTENANCE

Keep paper rush out of the weather and direct sunlight to maximize the lifespan of the seat. Dust and dirt can be vacuumed away. A protective clear coat can be added as necessary when the old coat starts to rub away.

DESIGN TIPS

Slots: Looks posh, but makes tensioning and proper compression difficult.

Curves: A little goes a long way. The deeper the curve, the more the material will slip. This applies to both concave and covex rails. Notching the rails helps keep the cord in its place on both types of curved edges.

Removable Seats: Keep it simple. Rectangles and trapezoids with block corners are your friends. Circles are the worst.

PRO TIP: *Restoring Rush Chair Sets*

When restoring multiple chairs, we weave them “production” style instead of weaving each chair from start to finish. Fill in the gussets of all the chairs in the set. Wrap each until they’re ready for cardboard. Cut cardboard for the whole set. Do all the sealing at once. It’s really a mind game, but whatever gets you through restoring seats for 10 rush chairs!

Listen to your body and take care of your hands, elbows, and shoulders. You may need tape for your fingers so you don’t get blisters.

CONTINENTAL WEAVE

When the side rail is longer than the back rail, the standard rush pattern results in a front-to-back bridge.

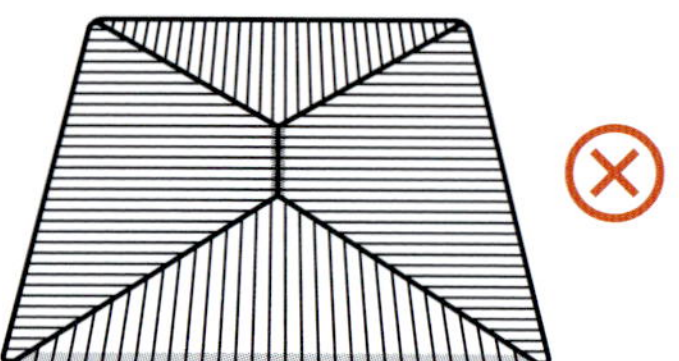

A front-to-back bridge is structurally unstable and uncomfortable.

The standard rush weave employs a 1:1 ratio of vertical/horizontal strands wrapping each corner.

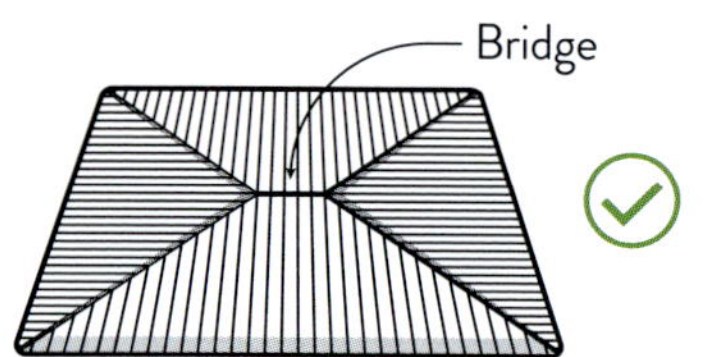

When the side rail is longer than the back rail, use the continental pattern to create a side-to-side bridge.

The continental weave increases that ratio by adding two or more strands to the side rails for every one strand on the front rail. The larger the ratio, the quicker the side rails fill up and the bridge drops further back.

You don't have to use the continental weave exclusively on deep seats. Try it for fun on your next rush project!

PRO TIP: ***Determine Bridge Length and Location***

As the weaver, you have control over the bridge location and length. Utilize larger continental weave ratios to drop the bridge farther back on the seat and lengthen it quickly.

When you reach your intended bridge length and/or location, finish with the standard 1:1 rush pattern.

- The bridge is located at the midpoint of the empty space on the side rails once the gussets are filled.
- The bridge length can be determined at any point in the weaving process by using the following equation:

Take measurements of the empty space along each rail:

X = Back Rail

Y = Side Rail

Z = Front Rail

B = Bridge Length

$$B = \frac{Z+X}{2} - Y$$

When B=0 the triangular quadrants meet at a point in the center.

When $B<0$; Vertical bridge and not ideal for comfort or structural integrity.

For a 2:1 ratio, add an extra side-to-side straightaway before making a corner and tacking on the right rail.

DANISH CORD RUSH

Danish Cord, a 3-ply paper twill, is found on several iconic Danish designs. It is available in unlaced and laced varieties and in diameters from ⅛" - 3⁄16". The laced version has an extra twist that adds visible texture, but is harder on your hands.

JH/PP550 Peacock Chair

J16 Rocker

CH24 Wishbone Chair

MATERIAL

When ordering cord, be aware that there is American cord and imported Danish cord. Spend extra for the Danish—at the time of writing, the quality is much better. Danish cord's density, coupled with slipperiness from the wax makes it tricky to tame. It will slip on the rails that are slightly bowed and on itself. It does not stretch or compress easily making adjusting difficult. Laced cord is harder on your hands than unlaced cord and gloves are worthwhile in both cases. Wrap the end with masking tape if tacking is difficult. Don't wet the Danish cord.

PROCESS

During manufacture, Danish rush seats are woven in a different pattern than the over-the-rail/up-the-middle method presented in "Paper Rush" and referenced in this section. For simplicity, we're opting not to introduce an entirely different weaving pattern. Short of dismantling the weave, the resulting seat is virtually indistinguishable from the original. Other differences that make Danish rush weaving unique include filling the gusset by wrapping the rail, weaving through slots, no cardboard added in between the woven layers and, often, there is no bridge.

DANISH CORD RUSH (CONTINUED)

1. Calculate and mark gussets. [Refer to Materials, Tools & Skills Library]

2. Pull off a coil of Danish cord that fits easily in the palm of your hand.

LEFT GUSSET

3. Tack the end of the Danish cord coil on the inside of the front rail ~2" from the left post. Tack again at the post.

4. Wrap the left side of the front rail tightly going over the rail and up the middle of the seat. Clamp on the back rail to compress the wraps. Keep wrapping/compressing until you reach the gusset mark.

5. Tack the cord on the inside of the left rail, close to the back, left post. Cut off the excess.

RIGHT GUSSET

6. Tack the end of the Danish cord coil on the inside of the front rail ~2" from the right post. Tack again at the post.

7. Wrap the right side of the front rail tightly going over the rail and up the middle of the seat. Clamp on the back rail to compress the wraps. Keep wrapping/compressing until you reach the gusset mark. *Do not tack and cut the excess material!*

8. Proceed with the standard rush pattern, using the rest of the coil. Adjust, compress and tie on new coils as necessary.
   - Proper tension is tricky. Maximum tension on the straightaway can over-tension the previous corner.
   - The waxed material can slip on the rail making compression difficult. Try wetting the rail without soaking the cord. The moisture will help hold the cord in place.
   - Don't over-adjust. Danish cord is slippery and doesn't respond well to lots of adjusting. If you have a troubling spot, it is better to back up and reweave.

SKILL // INTENTIONAL CORNERS

Ensure corners are halfway between offset rails. There are often large differences in the rail heights on Danish chairs.

Focus on lashing straightaways together when making a corner. Intentional corners don't require as much adjusting.

SKILL // NAVIGATING SLOTS

Don't start weaving through a slot as soon as you get to it. Weave up to ledges or spindles on the rail. Extra space in the slot allows the material to move and find its own equilibrium.

Compress in a slot using needle-nose pliers.

PRE-TWISTED NATURAL RUSH

Pre-twisted natural rush is a single-ply seagrass cord that mimics the look of hand-twisted bulrush and cattails. Museum pieces and historically significant chairs should be restored with authentic, hand-twisted cattail and bulrush whenever possible. Using a pre-twisted natural rush is the next best option. Pre-twisted natural rush is commonly available in sizes from 4⁄32" to 12⁄32". Similar to weaving with paper rush, smaller material is easier to work with but it takes longer to weave the seat. Weaving with pre-twisted natural rush is extra tedious due to its tendency to shred, untwist, and over-twist.

MATERIAL

Pre-twisted natural rush is stretchier than paper rush, but don't be fooled into thinking it will shrink when it dries. It can't be pulled as tight as paper rush or it will break. The material varies slightly in size. Avoid sections that are so thin that they lack structural integrity.

PREPARATION

Tape ends with masking tape before soaking to prevent unraveling. Soak coils in warm water for 10-15 minutes until you can manipulate the material without it feeling/sounding crunchy. Under-soaked material will break when wrapping it around the rail. Oversoaking results in slimy, untwisted material that is useless.

PROCESS

When tacking the gussets, wrap the ends in masking tape. Open up the material when making corners. Start early and you'll thank yourself in the end. The material naturally wants to spread apart in the middle of the pattern. Adding thickness when making a corner counteracts this tendency. The material is soft and compresses easily. Don't over-compress when making corner adjustments and compress lightly on the rails to prevent the "hourglass" effect mentioned in the paper rush section.

Beware of shredding material, especially when approaching and weaving the bridge. Once you begin pulling a single strand through the pattern, clamp the end of the strand to the chair to prevent untwisting. When pulling a single strand through, hold tension on both sides of the panel to tighten the cord, prevent kinks and minimize shredding. Clip fibers sticking out of new seat using small scissors or snips. Let dry overnight before sealing.

open material at corner

tight material at corner

TWISTED SEAGRASS

Twisted Seagrass is a 2-ply seagrass cord commonly available in sizes ⅛" to 5⁄16". Smaller sizes are easier to work with but it takes longer to weave the seat. Weaving with twisted seagrass is similar to weaving with paper rush and easier than pre-twisted natural rush because it doesn't shred as much. In addition to the rush pattern, the 2-ply cord works well for warp/weft weaving patterns commonly found woven in Danish cord.

MATERIAL

Twisted seagrass is very stretchy due to it being coiled like a spring. It varies in size along the length and sometimes has knots/kinks that should be avoided especially on top of the pattern.

PREPARATION

Soak coils in warm water for 10-15 minutes until you can manipulate the material without it feeling/sounding crunchy.

PROCESS

Pay special attention when pulling tension. On a straightaway, you can break the material if pulled too hard. Because the material is stretchy, it's easy to pull the pattern way out of 90° when tensioning the corners. Clip fibers sticking out of new seat using small scissors or snips. Let dry overnight before sealing.

INTRODUCTION TO HAND-TWISTED CORDS

CATTAIL & BULRUSH

Weaving with grasses is one of the more ancient weaving processes and is seen on chairs and stools from Ancient Egypt. Authentic rush is found on chairs by Gustav Stickley and Charles Rennie Mackintosh and most antique English ladder back chairs, some Windsor chairs, and American Hitchcock chairs. At one point in history the rush seats were coated with thick lead paint so they could be wipeable and longer lasting. While this is very practical, it does a disservice to the beauty of the hand-twisted seat.

I'd rather weave authentic cattails than paper or pre-twisted natural rush any day of the week if I had the time and space to harvest my own. Cathryn Peters of The Wicker Woman in the U.S. and Felicity Irons of Rushmatters in the U.K. are notable rush harvesters and weavers at the time this is written.

Bulrush and cattail rush are harvested annually in late summer when the tips of the grasses start to turn brown. Bulrush is most often used in the U.K. Cattails grow everywhere in the U.S. but the harvesting and curing process is so labor intensive, that few chair weavers take the time and effort. Those that do, save the rush for their own work and rightly so! The cattails are cut and dried in the sun, constantly being rotated to prevent rot and mold. After a few weeks they can be bundled and stored upright.

Cattail—Flat Profile

Bulrush—Round Profile

Hand-twisted Cattail—Top

Hand-twisted Cattail—Bottom

Manufactured Rush—Top

Manufactured Rush—Bottom

Photos on this page by Nathan Rivers Chesky.

Cattails have to mellow for several hours before weaving and should not be bent, so you'd need a large trough or a plastic tarp with a damp sheet on top. Spray/soak the leaves thoroughly and wrap with the sheet. You can tell if they are too dry because they crack when twisted. They should not be too wet and slimy. Once they are mellow you have to pop the cell walls. You can do this by running the back end of a knife down each strand and you'll hear pop-pop-pop! Or you can use a laundry crank and run several strands at a time through. It's messy work and it dries out and scratches your hands.

The basic pattern/process is similar to paper cord, wrapping four seat rails from corner posts to a bridge in the middle. New leaves are spliced in at the corners with the bulky lower stalks sticking below the seat. When weaving is finished the stalks below are clipped. The result is gorgeous ... soft but strong with natural color variations.

Museum pieces and historically significant chairs should be restored with authentic cattail and bulrush whenever possible. Weaving with pre-twisted natural rush is the next best option (due to lack of availability in the U.S.) and it is reversible. The chair police will arrest you if you put paper rush on historically significant chairs. You can see the difference in manufactured rush vs. cattails or bullrush on the bottom of the seat but it is nearly indistinguishable on top.

INTRODUCTION TO HAND-TWISTED CORDS (CONTINUED)

CORN SHUCKS

Corn shucks are one of the few traditionally North American materials (corn comes from Mexico). I am IN LOVE with corn shuck chairs. They are the longest lasting seats. And not the easiest to weave. The chair frames of the corn shuck chairs I've encountered are well crafted for comfort, and typically made by people who did not have advanced degrees in design from Rhode Island School of Design or other fine woodworking schools.

Modern harvesting can only be done in small fields where combines don't shred the fibers. Red field corn creates a lovely candy cane stripe. They are spliced and twisted together in a similar manner as authentic cattails and bulrush. Whereas the grass leaves are ideally 6'-10', the corn shuck "leaves" are about 6" long. It takes a lot of material to weave the seat and several days per chair. The corn shucks are soaked, not too dry, not too soggy. You can only use the middle third of the shuck: The outermost bits are too thick and the inner bits are too flimsy. As with other weaving materials, the patterns vary. In addition to the rush pattern, corn shuck chairs are also woven in a warp/weft method, some distinctive to a particular region of the Southeastern U.S., like the diamonds on Gatlinburg chairs and footstools. At the time of writing, only a few people in the U.S. weave with corn shucks. We are indebted to David Russell of Washington, Ga., for sharing his knowledge, skills, and shucks.

Chair and stool by Don Ward, part of Arrowmont's collection.

Hunter Rocker—from the collection of Dave Lindsay.

Irish wrap with corn shucks part of Silver River Chairs collection.

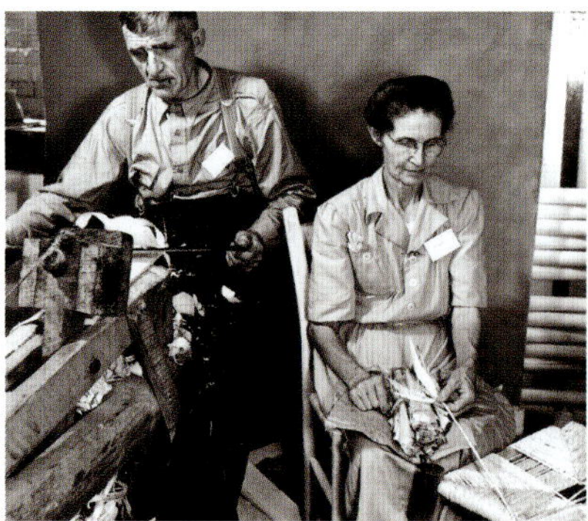

Southern Highland Craft Guild—Birdie & Sara Mace

Sara Mace twisting corn shucks at Craft Fair of the Southern Highlands.

CORDON RUSH, AKA WHEAT WRAP

Yet another niche material, cordon rush is very finicky to work with. It is typically found on French chairs. Denis Guérin in La Rochelle, France, creates stunning masterpieces weaving with straw polychromy. His work is a feast for the eyes. We've seen a lot of French cordon rush chairs and we have seen the quality of the manufactured cordon rush go down over the years. Do your best with the manufactured stuff. See you in France for a class with Denis!

Traditional cordon rush on antique French chair

Images courtesy of Denis Guerin

MID-CENTURY CHAIR DESIGN 101

Mid-Century Modern Design in the 20th century had an important impact on chair weaving and chairmaking. The designers emphasized natural wood finishes, created bold structural innovations, and devised new methods of weaving classic materials like rattan and paper cord. Ladderback chairs, Windsor chairs, and the classic yoke-back Asian chair designs were updated and, dare I say, improved upon? At the time of writing, designs of this era, both authentic and imitations, are highly desirable.

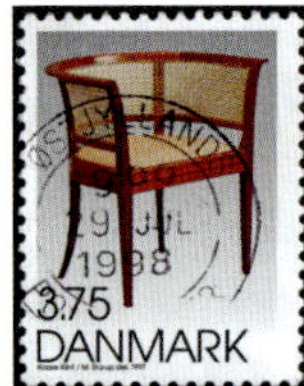

The Faaborg chair started the design revolution known as Danish Modernism and Kaare Klint (1888-1954) is known as the father of the movement. The Faaborg Chair was designed in 1914, 10-15 years before Marcel Breuer and Mies Van der Rohe designed their iconic chairs. A curved, hand-woven cane back with either a caned seat or upholstered with leather became the model for utilizing clean lines, hand-polished wood, and woven elements in seats and backs. It was honored with a postage stamp in the 1990s.

Nathan Rivers Chesky

Mies Van der Rohe (MR20 Armchair)

Laced (left) and unlaced (right) Danish cord comparision.

Many Mid-century chairs have corded seats and/or backs. Danish cord, a 3-ply paper twill, embodies the design elements of strength, simplicity and elegance. The material is waxed during the manufacturing process for added strength and ease of weaving. It is available in unlaced and laced varieties and in diameters from ⅛" - 3/16". The laced version has an extra twist that adds texture.

We can't discuss Danish chair design without Hans Wegner and Niels Otto Møller of Denmark. Wegner borrowed elements of centuries old chair designs, expanded and elevated them, making the weaving more complicated, the seats more interesting, by adding slots to rush chairs and ornamental wrapping with binder cane. Many of his designs incorporate Danish cord in either

George Nakashima chair and stool restored by Brandy Clements and Dave Klingler.

rush or warp/weft patterns, but he really shined with his unique use of binder cane: The Chair (501) and the JH-512 Folding Chair, etc. This chair inspired the Yugoslavian Folding Chair, which is more common.

Møller's iconic designs are notable in their elegantly highlighting wood grain, often in teak but occasionally in rosewood. The seats are typically Danish cord but are also found in upholstered leather and binder cane. Despite designs being similar throughout the body of work, the excitement comes with the multitude of nuanced chair backs ... which is, after all, what we see when they are in use.

Scandinavian designs have been imitated, for better or worse, since they came into being. These reproductions are usually less comfortable, but still attractive with smooth, natural wood finishes and woven seats. Not all imitations fall short of the goals of Danish design and reflect their simplicity and excellence.

Hallmarks of imitations are triangular braces at the posts, staples instead of L-nails and a less contoured seat. Authentic chairs have a comfortable curve at the front and back rails with straight side rails with a rounded profile. Look for other maker's marks. We've seen "Danish" designs with "Made in Japan," "Made in Indonesia," "Made in Yugoslavia," etc. The "Yugoslavian Folding Chair" is a common enough design that we are including detailed instructions in this instructional manual. Be aware that some Danish manufacturers do use staples instead of L-nails and we've seen Swedish designs with round headed nails. So many chairs! All so different!

Thailand danish cord chair.

Thailand Danish cord seat corner braces.

Mid-Century Swedish split-rail chair.

MØLLER NO. 79 PROJECT & SIMILAR CHAIRS

// TIME: ~4-6 HOURS //

Danish cord first became widely used in Scandinavian chair designs of the 1950s and '60s. Notably (but certainly not exclusively) were chairs by Niels Otto Møller of Denmark. We are using Møller No. 79 for this project.

Møller chairs and their cousins are woven in a warp/weft method. Pairs of Danish cord span the front and back rails, leaving gaps that are filled in by wrapping cord around the rails. The pattern is completed by weaving the weft through the gaps and wrapping around the side rails in an over/under basket weave.

The innovative design of widening the rails and using L-shaped nails to hook the warp and weft results in only one panel of weaving vs. a top and bottom layer. The weaver doesn't have to pull a giant handful of material through two layers of patterns on top and bottom. You only pull enough cord off of the spool to get across and hook on a nail. It cuts weaving time in half and with an additional ergonomic bonus: you don't need to turn the chair upside down every row.

Møller 56 Armchair

Møller 71 Side Chair

Refer to Materials, Tools & Skills Library for more detailed information.

**** Denotes tools that are helpful, but optional.***

TOOLS

Needle-nose Pliers

Wire Snips

Scissors/Utility Knife

Small Hammer

Flathead Screwdriver

Rasp/Sandpaper

6" Spring Clamp

Claw Tool*

Nail Set*

MATERIALS

Laced or Unlaced Danish Cord

L-Nails

Masking Tape*

BASIC SKILLS

Compressing on the Rail

Inchworm Technique

Using a Ramp

Clamping

Danish Cord: The standard Møller chair requires ~2 lb of Danish cord. Danish cord is commonly available in 2 lb coils and in 10-11 lb spools. Plan to have extra cord on hand in case you run short. At the time of writing, both American-made cord and imported Danish cord are available. The imported cord is slightly larger and a superior product. Either laced cord (more texture) or unlaced cord (smoother) can be used. We find the unlaced variety slightly easier to work with. Fair warning: You will get arrested by the chair police for using paper rush on Danish cord chairs!

L-Nails: It's good to have a few extra nails on hand in case the original nails break or are missing. Not all L-nails are created equal. We prefer stamped nails that have a flat surface to hammer against. Please don't use staples on chairs created for L-nails. It's usually not worth the effort to replace staples with L-nails on frames intended to be stapled. L-nails are available at most suppliers.

Chair Frame: At the time of writing this book, authentic Møller chair frames are desirable and costly. Møller chairs have chunky rails to accommodate tons of L-nails. Other similar designs may have L-nails, staples or round-headed nails. Some chair frames have the typical chunky front and back rails with the L-nails but have two side rails on each side where the cord is woven in a figure eight and not hooked on a nail at all. Weaving instructions for the "split rail" Danish cord chair frames are at the end of this section.

BEFORE YOU WEAVE

Take a before photo of the chair! It's fun to see before and after. You may not want to use the previous seat as a guide—the previous weaver could have made mistakes.

Remove the old seat. Cut all of the "pairs" along the front and back rails. Cut along the inside of the side rails. If using a blade, a sawing motion works best. Don't cut the material on the rail and damage the rail with the knife blade. Work from the posts to the middle, rotate the chair and repeat. This helps avoid accidentally cutting the post. Pry open all L-nails. Nails may bend, break, pull out slightly, or pull out entirely. Remove material from L-nails. Unwrap front and back rails.

Repair any structural issues. [Refer to Structural Issues & Repairs]

Repair loose/broken joints: Because these chairs do not usually have stretchers to support the posts, the joints are under extra pressure. Multiple tenons compound the issue and cracks in the front posts are common. If you can get the joint apart, it's best to clean up the old glue and reglue/clamp as necessary. With a hairline crack, CA glue is a better choice. When using a strap clamp, make sure it runs in line with the rails for a snug fit.

Roll over sharp edges: The front and back rails are usually sharp at the inside edge and that is a common area for cord breaks to occur. Roll the edges over slightly with a rasp or sandpaper to extend the life of the new seat.

Adding/replacing L-nails: Nails can be missing, broken or need relocating. You can usually reuse existing holes, but if you are adding a nail, make sure to drill a pilot hole first. The pilot hole will make it much easier to hammer home and reduce the pressure that the nail is putting on the rail.

Cracked rail due to nails: If the original nails were lined up too close to a woodgrain line or pilot holes weren't large enough, the rail can crack. Back out all the nails→drip CA glue into the crack(s)→clamp over night→redrill pilot holes and replace nails.

Prepare the chair frame. Wipe down the frame. We use Howard Feed-N-Wax to nourish and protect the wood. Don't oil the seat rails.

WARP & WRAP THE FRONT RAIL

We prefer to simultaneously wrap the front rail while lacing the doubled warp strands. This method is derived from reverse-engineering Hans Wegner chairs and differs from the conventional Møller method.

1 Make ~1 lb coil for the warp strands and the wrapping of the front rail. Keep the coil in its natural shape to avoid a tangly mess.

> **PRO TIP:**
> *Material Wrangling*
>
> Use a clamp or twist tie to prevent coiled material from unspooling off the work table.

2 Zigzag the loose end of the 1 lb coil through the L-shaped nails on the left rail.

3 Wrap the cord under the front rail, across the seat, over the back rail and hook it onto the first nail in the back rail.

4 Wrap the cord under the back rail, across the seat, over the front rail and hook it onto the first nail in the front rail. Keep the tension equal to the first warp strand.

> **SKILL // WARP TENSION**
>
> Warp strands do not need to be tight. The weaver strands will take up any extra slack. Aim for just shy of taut with a little undulation in the strand. The most important aspect is to keep similar tension across all of the warp strands.

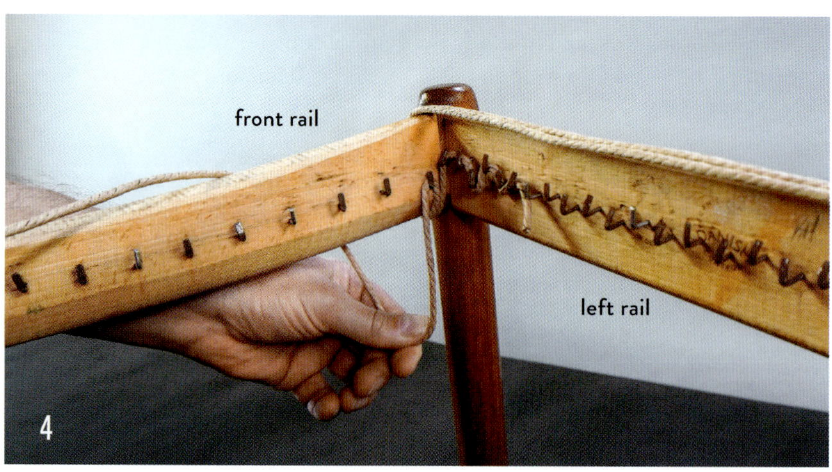

SKILL // COMPRESSING MATERIAL

For a uniform seat, aim to get the maximum amount of material on the rails. Use a screwdriver like a paddle and tap it with a hammer, compressing the Danish cord and making space for more material. Back off of your compression if the strands start to double-up. Compression is necessary for both the warp and the weaver strands.

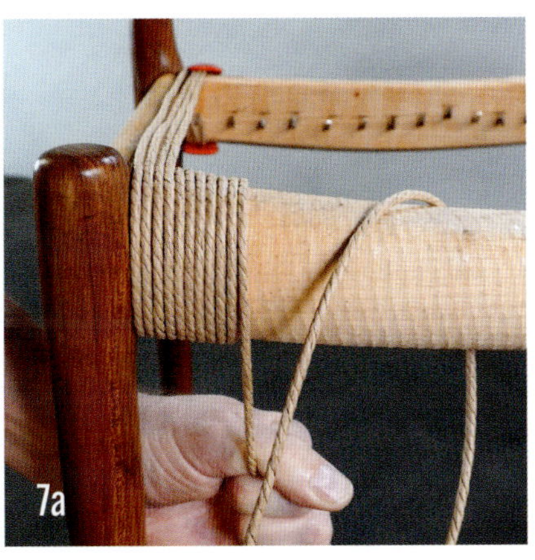

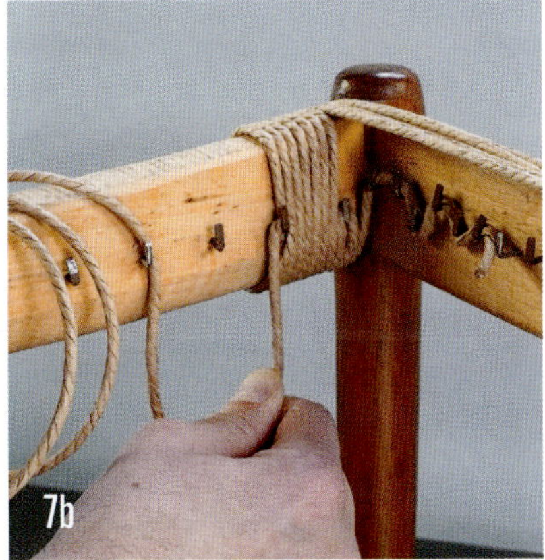

5 Wrap the cord under the front rail, across the seat, over the back rail and hook it onto the first nail in the back rail. There will be two loops on the one nail, so make sure that the cord crosses over inside the back rail and not visibly. Keep the tension equal to previous strands. You will now have four warp strands next to the side rail.

6 Wrap the entire coil 6-8 times, loosely around the front rail. Always work the coil over the rail and UP the middle of the seat. Typically, there are 5-6 wraps in between nails, but the extra wraps will become a warp pair and start the front-rail wraps in the next sequence.

7 Tighten the wraps until you are touching the next nail. With the next wrap, hook the nail.

WARP & WRAP THE FRONT RAIL (CONTINUED)

8 Compress the wraps. If you can fit another wrap after compressing, wrap one more loop and rehook the material on the nail.

9 Wrap the material over the back rail and hook the next nail. The warp pairs on the back rail won't be locked into position until the back rail is wrapped later in the process.

10 Continue wrapping the front rail and adding warp pairs until you hook the second to last nail on the front rail. Don't forget to compress as you go.

11 Wrap the front rail and compress until there is space for four warp strands. Focus your compression on the bottom of the rail; the bottom rail fills up more quickly than the top.

12 Mirror the initial set of four warp strands by wrapping the cord under the rails, across the top of the seat, and hooking it on the last nail in the front/back rails. Remember that there will be two loops on the one nail, so make sure that the cord crosses over inside the rail and not visibly.

13 Wrap the final warp strand over/under the front rail and loop it tightly over the first nail on the right rail and secure coil with a twist-tie.

9

10

11a

11b

11c

13

WRAP THE BACK RAIL

15

PRO TIP: *Squeezing in one more strand*

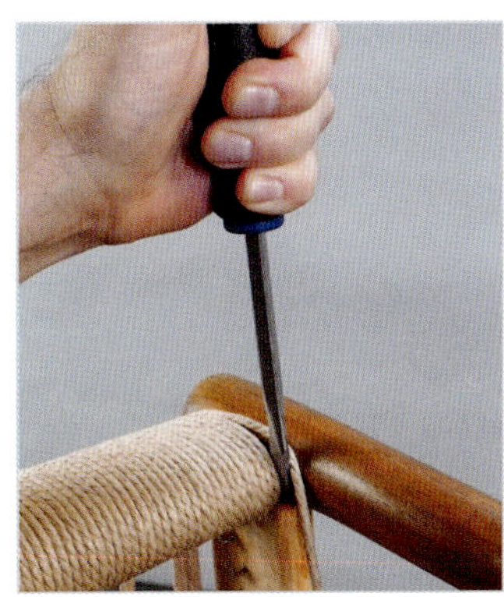

Work the screwdriver into the gap on the rail. Pull the cord between the screwdriver and the post, wedging it without risking damage to the frame.

14 Cut off 14 yards of cord to wrap the back rail.

15 Zigzag one end of the cord through the L-nails at the back of one side rail.

16 Wrap the coil loosely around the back rail between the four warp strands and the first warp strand pair. There are typically 4-5 wraps between warp pairs.

17 Tighten the wraps and compress on the rail. Fill the space between the nails completely. Add or remove wraps as necessary. Don't cross over the nail when you move from one wrapped section to the next. The strands should lay flush against the inside of the rail.

17a

17b

WRAP THE BACK RAIL (CONTINUED)

18 Continue to wrap between the warp strands until you reach the other side. Use a clamp to hold tension in the wraps.

19 End with ~4" zigzag through the nails and cut off any excess cord.

Tao of Chair: Find Your Path

Sometimes wrapping with a coil works great. Sometimes wrapping one strand at a time and pulling the full length through works great. Choose what works for you in the moment.

18

19a

19b

WEAVING THE WEFT

The weft is woven over and under the warp strands in a double row of cord, cinching it on the L-nails as you go. Weaving the one panel is so much simpler than weaving a top and bottom layer. You don't have to bring a huge coil of cord over and under each warp strand ... just enough to get across and you don't have to turn the chair over every row!

20

21

22

20 Pull a double-length of material out of the coil. Make sure it will make it all the way across the seat.

21 Take the loop and weave over the first set of four warp strands. Weave under and over alternately until you reach the other side. The pattern is symmetrical and you weave over the last set of four warp strands like the first.

22 Pull SLIGHT tension on the loop. This first strand will want to be "straight" and you want to force it to be slightly "serpentine."

23 Hook the nail closest to the front rail and bring the first cord's mate across the seat without adding tension. Hook the opposite nail closest to the front rail. The first weft pair is tensioned loosely on the nails.

WEAVING THE WEFT (CONTINUED)

24 Weave the second weft pair through the pattern, starting under the first set of four warp strands. The weaving pattern alternates as you move up the seat. Specific tensioning skills for the rest of the seat are outlined in the "Skills" section.

25 Continue to weave pairs through the warp strands, weaving over/under opposite to the previous strands. Keep the weft strands perpendicular to the side rails with no bowing toward the front or back rails. Compress with a hammer and screwdriver on the side rails every few pairs. The warp pairs tend to shift side to side as you weave and should be tweaked side-to-side if necessary.

24

25

SKILL // STARTING/STOPPING WEAVER STRANDS

At the end of a strand, zigzag the end through ~3" of the nails on the side rail. Clip excess material. Start another coil with a zigzag through the nails on the opposite side rail. Staggering the ends leaves more room for weaver loops on the nails. It's OK to end and start with a single strand of a pair.

SKILL // WEFT TENSION

Proper tension is important and it's not as tight as you might think. Authentic Danish chairs have curved front and back rails and you want the seat to follow the curve. Too much tension, visible as a flat or convex seat surface, puts undue stress on joints that aren't supported by lower stretchers.

Pull tight in the direction you are weaving and let the loop hang loose. Start at the last anchor point and push the strand into the pattern without adding more tension. You are aiming for serpentine weaver strands that are barely touching each other. Too much tension also prevents the weft strands from being pushed close together.

PRO TIP: *Material Wrangling*

Significantly reduce the amount of under/over twists in the material by using a spinning platform. Unwind the Danish cord from the outside of the spool. Make sure there is a center post to keep the spool from falling over.

SKILL // CHOOSING A NAIL

Although there are usually two strands per nail, sometimes it's three and sometimes it's one. Look straight down over the side rail. If you can still see the nail, use it. If the nail is covered by the weft strands, ignore it. Compress on the side rails regularly to ensure that you are choosing nails wisely. Ultimately, the loops on the inside of the side rails should be vertical or leaning slightly toward the front of the chair.

Only use "visible" nails.

SKILL // HOOKING A NAIL

Pull the working strand down and taut against the outside of the side rail without adding tension to the weave. Loop it onto the chosen nail while keeping the tension you created. Pull the cord down firmly and tight against the nail. If the nail tries to spin, hold it in place with needle-nose pliers. It seems simple, but if you don't properly tension on the nails, the material on the side rails looks lumpy due to excess slack.

WEAVING THE WEFT (CONTINUED)

26a

26b

26 When approaching the back posts, compress the material on the side rails forcefully to wedge as many pairs onto the rails as possible. You can weave the loop halfway through the chair, pull tension and then weave the other half. **[a]** Or, you can weave one over-under at a time. If you have less than 1" of empty rail, determine the approximate length (plus some extra!) cord needed to finish weaving. Cut extra length off of your weaving coil and weave one strand at a time instead of two. **[b]** The rear rail/post joint is often angled and it's OK if there is a slight gap on the bottom of the rail when the top is completely full.

PRO TIP: *Squeeze in One More Strand*

Work in one more strand by placing the screwdriver into the gap on the rail. Pull the cord between the screwdriver and the post, wedging it without risking damage to the frame.

FINISHING THE CHAIR

27a

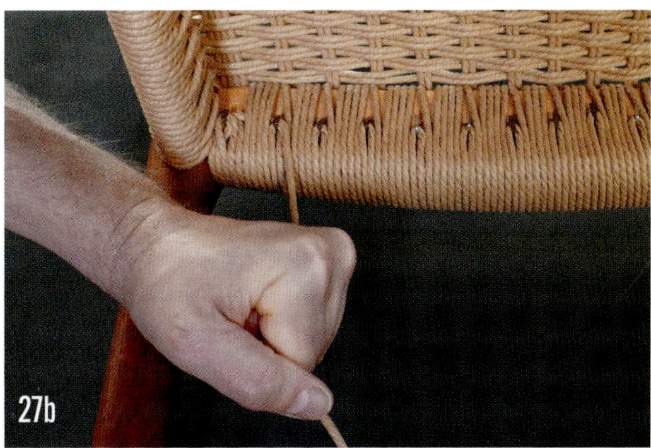
27b

27c

28

27 Pull the loose end taught on the side rail. Hook it on the first nail on the back rail. Slide the strand under the first set of wraps using a tool to make space. Pull the strand taught and hook it on the second nail on the back rail. Reseat the second nail with a hammer, making sure the rail is supported. Clip off excess material to complete the process.

28 Reseat the L-nails by hammering them back into the rail or bending them to secure the cord loops. Use a support block to prevent bouncing and rail damage. A nail set is helpful when working close to the posts.

FINISHING THE CHAIR (CONTINUED)

29 Adjust the seat for uniformity by moving weaver pairs forward/backward as necessary. Aim for small gaps at the front and back rails and little-to-no space in between the weaver pairs.

30 Give yourself a high-five or do a little dance! Give your seat a little drum tap, hug the chair, whatever feels good. The gratification of finishing a chair project never gets old.

front rail

side rail

MAINTENANCE

Danish cord chairs are indoor chairs! An occasional vacuuming works to remove dirt from between the cords. Danish cord is treated with wax to reduce staining, but spills can discolor it. We don't recommend spot cleaning, but according to the Carl Hansen website, it's possible to clean Danish cord with a mild, natural soap solution on an almost-dry cloth. This should be done sparingly or it will damage the cord. Avoid synthetic detergents.

DESIGN TIPS

Chair designs using L-nails require large rails made of hardwood. Traditionally, European beech is used and rails are at least 2"-3" tall and ¾" thick. Maple is a good substitute for beech for those of us on the other side of the pond where beech is a little harder to come by. A curved profile on the outside of the front/back rails helps prevent baggy-looking rail-wraps. Avoid sharp edges on any of the rails.

Whether converting an upholstered Danish chair or designing a new build, L-nail placement is the key to success. Map the layout onto all the rails first, drill pilot holes and then hammer the L-nails in partially.

Front/Back Rails: Traditionally, when laying out the front/back rails, there is a nail for each set of four warp strands on either end and 15 additional pairs of two warp strands equidistant from each other for a total of 17 nails on both the front and the back rails. Mark the midline of the rail→Mark the center nail at the exact center of the rail, slightly above the midline→Mark the end nails ¼" from the post and slightly below the midline→Measure the distance between the center nail and the end nail and divide by 8→Mark that distance between the remaining nails at the midline of the rail (it's helpful to work you way from the center nail mark and the end nail mark, meeting in the middle)→Adjust marks as needed to be as equidistant as possible→drill pilot holes at each mark. The number of pairs and the distance between can be altered to suit your design dimensions.

Side Rails: Mark the midline of the rail→mark every ½" along the midline→drill pilot holes at each mark while alternating distances above and below the midline to prevent cracking the rail along the grain.

Front/Back Rail Layout—Danish Nails
Locate nails equidistant along the midline.

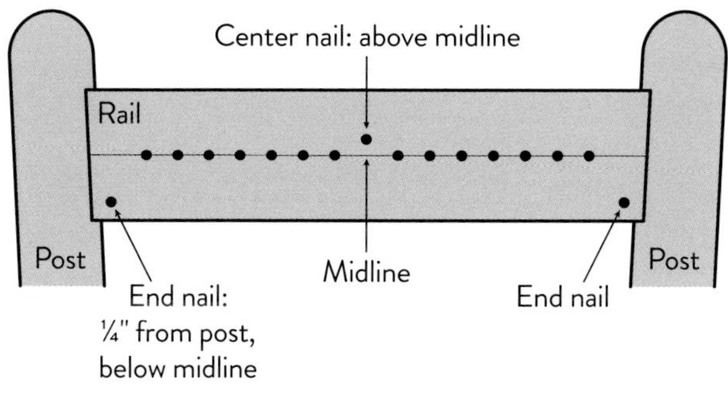

Side Rail Layout—Danish Nails
No set number of holes per chair

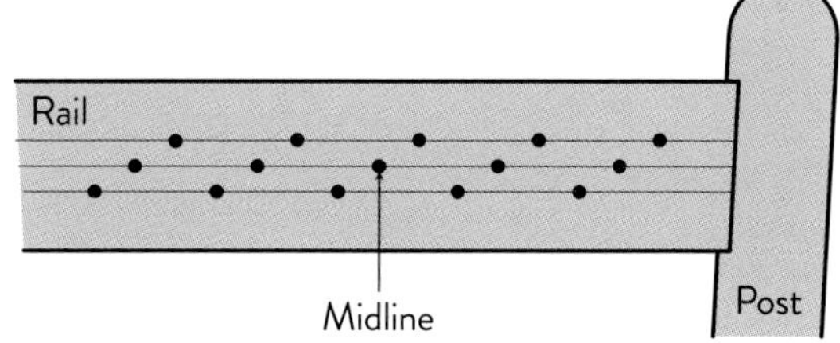

Nail holes approximately ½" apart equidistant and scattered above/below the center line randomly

DANISH CORD ON SPLIT-RAIL DESIGNS

The Wegner CH23 has an ornamental "Wrapped Pair" pattern on the side rails. The weaving pattern is the same as Møller chairs, but instead of hooking on nails, the cord is wrapped around and through the split rails.

WARP & RAIL WRAPS

L-nails on the inside of the front/back rails allow for the same warp wrapping method as a standard Møller chair. Because of the difference in the front/back rail construction, additional nails are necessary to create the double-pair of warp strands on either side of the seat. These nails are on the bottom of the front and back rails instead of inside.

1 Start on the front rail, tacking/stapling the end of ~1 lb cord in the nook next to the front post. Use the nails on the bottom of the front and back rails to create the first double warp pair. Wrap the front rail and add warp pairs until there is only space for four strands. Use the nails on the bottom of the rails as you did at the beginning to create the final double warp pair. End with a tack on the inside nook.

1a front rail, left side

1b front rail, right side

2 For the back rail wrap, start with a tack on the ledge by the nook. Wrap the rail between the warp pairs and end with a tack on the opposite side. You may need to staple the outermost wraps on either side to keep them from sliding into the nooks.

2 back rail

Refer to the Møller #79 section for instructions on warp pairs and wraps.

5

WEAVING THE WEFT

The double-strands will try to cross over each other. Make sure they are not crossed before tensioning and moving on. Make liberal use of a clamp to hold the tension while you are wrapping the rails. Don't forget to compress the material to ensure you pack as much material on the frame as possible.

3 Start with a comfortable amount of Danish cord ~15-20 yds. It's a balance: Excessive material knots up as you weave—less material means more splicing.

4 Fold the cord almost in half, creating a double-strand with the ends a yard or two apart. Both ends of the double-strand will need to be spliced onto new strands with a knot. Ideally, those knots won't end up next to each other.

5 Hook the "almost-center" of the double-strand on the side rail at one of the front posts.

6 Wrap the double-strand around both side rails and weave across the seat. Go over the four strands, then under/over until you go over the four strands at the opposite side. Bring the doubled cord around both rails on this side. This creates the first "pairs" fully around both of the side rails. Do not pull tight and raise the warp strands.

7 Loosely wrap the double-strand around the lower rail twice. Tighten the wrap on the lower rail and clamp.

8 Bring the loose end around the top rail and weave through the pattern opposite the first pair. You have created the first "shadow-pair" on one side.

7

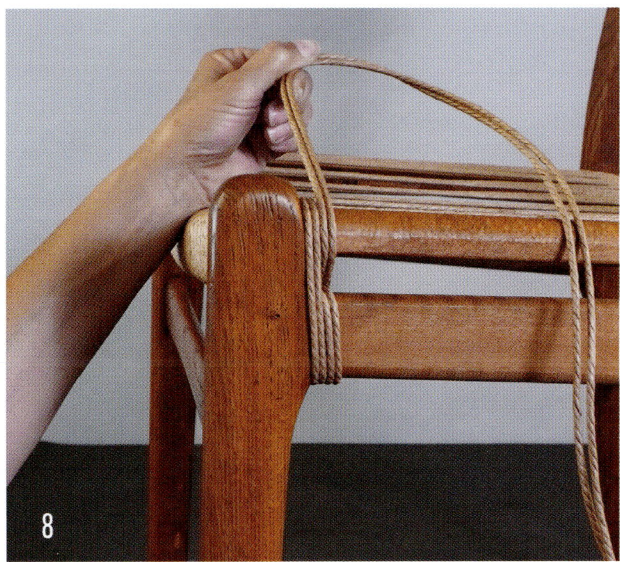
8

DANISH CORD ON SPLIT-RAIL DESIGNS (CONTINUED)

9 Back on the first side, the double-strand comes over the top rail and through the split rails. Then up and around the lower rail creating the matching shadow-pair on the first side. Pull taut on the lower rail wrap and clamp.

10 Repeat Steps 4-7. Compress the material on the rails as you weave and splice on a new strand when necessary.

For aesthetics and symmetry, start and end the pattern with a visible "pair" and not a "shadow-pair." Secure the ends of the double-strand with tacks/staples or loop them onto a Danish nail and hammer the nail in.

9

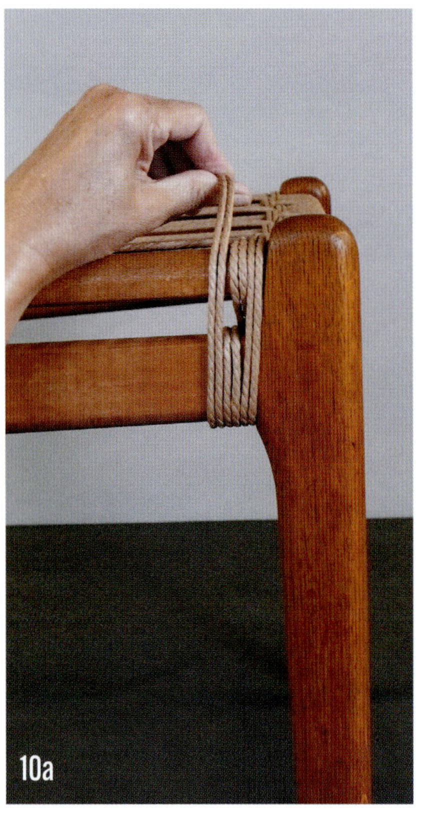
10a

10b

SKILL // SPLICING

Attach a new strand to the ending strand using a square knot.

- Splice one strand at a time so the knots don't crowd each other.
- Hide the knot on the inside of the side rail. You can clip the ends close to the knot or tuck the ends under a few rail wraps first.

DESIGN TIPS

The "Wrapped Pair" method isn't limited to Wegner designs and can be used to accent any frame with double rails.

SKILL // TWISTS

- Watch for twists inside the rail, inside the figure eight, and within the pattern!
- You don't have to unweave the pattern completely. Loosen the cord until you have enough slack to fix the twist.

YUGOSLAVIAN FOLDING CHAIR PROJECT

// TIME: 10-15 HOURS //

Although we refer to the following project as the "Yugoslavian Folding Chair," similar folding chairs were made in Japan, Italy, etc. These folding chairs are often referred to as "Wegner Style" although they were not actually designed by him. Subtle differences in design are evident. The Japanese version is particularly tedious with each weft strand on the back being invisibly tacked onto the post. Look carefully and you can usually find a stamp that indicates country of origin. This particular frame has a small, indistinct "Yugoslavia" stamp.

The Hans Wegner design (JH512) that inspired the iconic Yugoslavian Folding Chair is woven with rattan. A more common chair "out in the wild," the Yugslavian Folding Chair was woven with a braided cord. Danish cord is an appropriate substitute material. We recommend weaving the official Wegner versions with rattan as they were intended.

No matter what version of the chair you encounter, the basic pattern is woven in a warp/weft method with pairs of warp strands spanning the front and back rails. Gaps in between the warp pairs are filled by wrapping cord around the rails. The pattern is completed by weaving the weft through the warp and wrapping around the side rails in an over/under basket weave. For this project, the warping process will be the same for the seat and back. Then, we take the opportunity presented by the two separate panels to introduce two different methods of weaving the weft. You can choose one or mix and match as you see fit.

Courtesy of David Johnson, Sidecar Furniture

Wegner JH512

Yugoslavia makers mark

Refer to Materials, Tools & Skills Library for more detailed information.

**** Denotes tools that are helpful, but optional.***

TOOLS

Needle-nose Pliers

Scissors/Utility Knife/Snips

Hammer

Flathead screwdriver

Spring Clamp (x2)

Pencil

Ruler/Tape Measure

Nail Set*

MATERIALS

Laced or Unlaced Danish Cord

Masking Tape

Tacks

BASIC SKILLS

Using a Ramp

Inchworm Technique

Clamping

Tacking

Compressing on the Rails

BEFORE YOU WEAVE

Danish Cord: A full restoration of both the seat and back requires ~6 lb of Danish cord. Danish cord is commonly available in 2 lb coils and 10-11 lb spools. 6 lb should be plenty of material, but plan to have extra cord on hand so you don't run short. At the time of writing, there are both American-made cord and imported Danish cord available. The imported cord is slightly larger and a superior product. Either laced cord (more texture) or unlaced cord (smoother) can be used. We find the unlaced easier to work with and use it unless a specific request is made.

Take a before photo of the chair! It's fun to see before and after. You may or may not want to use the previous seat as a guide. If we like the spacing, we use it as a template for the replacement seat.

Mark previous pair groupings in the center of each middle pair. Do this on the top of both seat rails and on the front of the back rails. Some patterns (the back of this project) require an odd number of pair groupings. You may need to adjust your markings to add or reduce the number of groupings.

Remove the old seat. Use a blade, snips, or scissors to cut through the old material. Don't cut on the rail and damage the wood. Unwrap any loose bits and vacuum the decades of dust that manage to cling to the frame.

Repair any structural issues. Glue loose joints and tighten loose hinge brackets. [Refer to Structural Issues & Repairs]

Prepare the chair frame. Wipe down the frame and inspect the finish. The clear-coat on these chairs is often dry, cracked and peeling. You can weave as-is, take some time to nourish the wood or fully refinish the frame. For this project, we used a card scraper to remove the clear coat, applied Howard Restor-A-Finish (Golden Oak) and followed that with Howard Feed-N-Wax. Don't add finish or wax to the areas of the rail where there will be cord.

To aid in folding, *wax the track* that the wooden support piece slides along.

WRAPPING THE WARP—SEAT & BACK

The following instructions are written for the seat, but the process is the same for both the seat and back. A change in orientation is the only difference. Seat (Front and Back Rails) = Back (Bottom and Top Rails). Note: The alternate weaving pattern we chose to use on the back requires an odd number of pair groupings. The previous version had an even number, so we added a grouping, and adjusted the initial marks, making sure they were evenly spaced.

1 Make two coils of cord ~1 lb each. Keep them in their natural shape to avoid a tangly mess. Use a twist-tie on each coil to prevent them slinking off the work table.

2 Tack the end of one coil on the inside of the back rail ~1" from the side rail. Tack again at the corner on the back rail to hold the end in place. Originally, the manufacturer didn't tack the end and used the wraps to hold the end in place. We prefer to use tacks to save some fumbling.

3 Wrap the coil loosely 5-6 times around the back rail. Wrap under the rail, up the outside of the rail and down the inside of the rail.

4 Tighten and compress the wraps, adding more until there is space for three strands between the compressed wraps and the first center-mark.

5 Bring the back coil across the seat and clamp on the front rail, 6"-8" from the side rail, creating a gap at the back rail between the wraps and the strand coming forward.

SKILL //
COMPRESSING MATERIAL

Use a hammer and flathead screwdriver to get the most amount of material on the rails. [Refer to Materials, Tools & Skills Library]

PRO TIP:
Pneumatic Stapler

To save time and effort, use a pneumatic stapler instead of tacks. We use an upholstery stapler that shoots a 23 gauge, 3/16" crown staple in varying leg lengths.

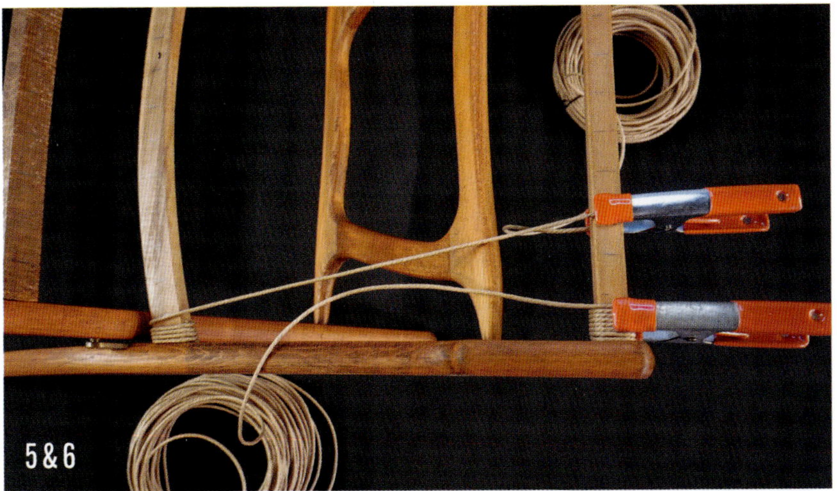
5&6

6 Repeat Steps 2-4 on the front rail and clamp the wraps on the front rail.

7 Bring the front-rail coil across the seat and around the back rail. Thread the coil between the working strand and the side rail.

Tighten the strand while staying in the gap on the back rail created by the first warp strand. There will be one wrap between the working strand and the warp pair on the inside of the rail.

7

SKILL // WARP TENSION

Warp strands should be taut. Most importantly, pull comfortable tension that you're able to keep uniform across all of the strands.

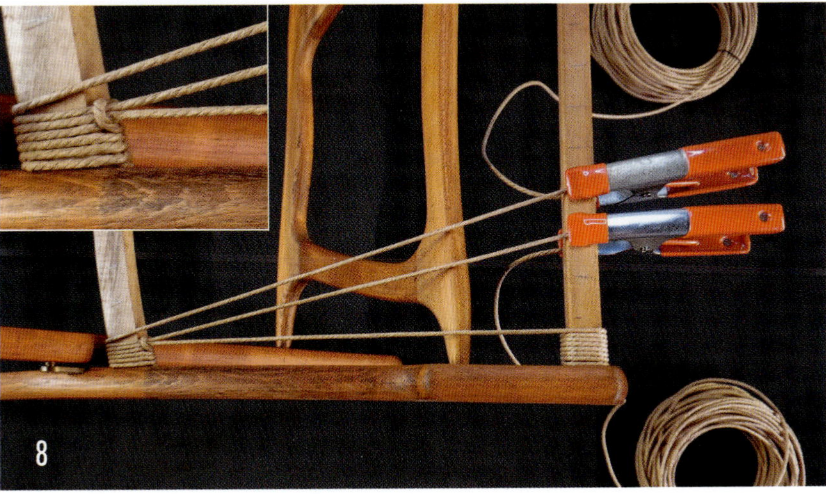
8

8 Create a bead over the two warp strands by wrapping the working coil over the warp pair (and the single wrap). Continue to wrap under/around the back rail and bring the coil to the front, clamping on the front rail slightly down from the initial clamped coil.

WRAPPING THE WARP—SEAT & BACK (CONTINUED)

9 Unclamp and bring the initial coil over so you have two strands side by side at the front. Wrap the initial coil under/around the front rail and bring the coil up on the "wrapped" side of the rail.

10 Create the bead at the front rail by wrapping the coil over the warp pair (and NO wraps). Bring it under/around the front rail and clamp it.

11 Rough in the next warp pair and beading *before you add tension.*

Wrap the working strand/coil loosely over the back rail, between the first warp pair and the new warp pair. Create the second bead at the back rail by wrapping the strand/coil over the new warp pair and under the back rail.

At the front rail, wrap the second strand/coil between the first warp pair and the new warp pair, over the new warp pair and under the front rail, creating the second bead bead.

9

10

11

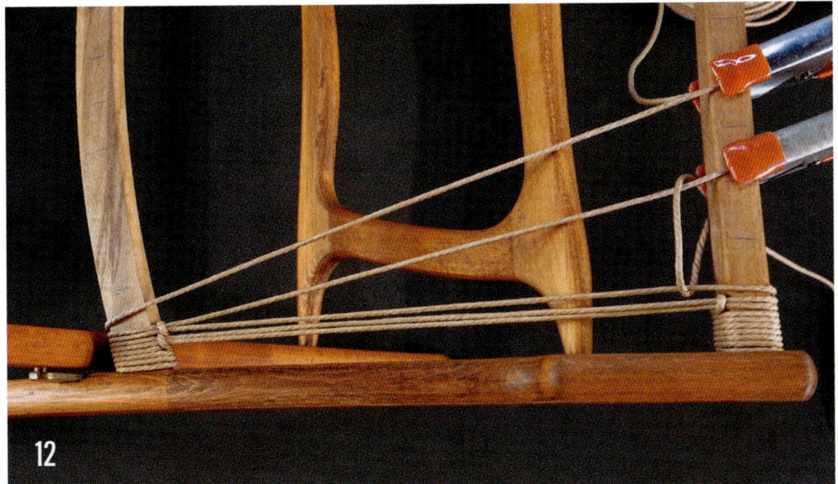
12

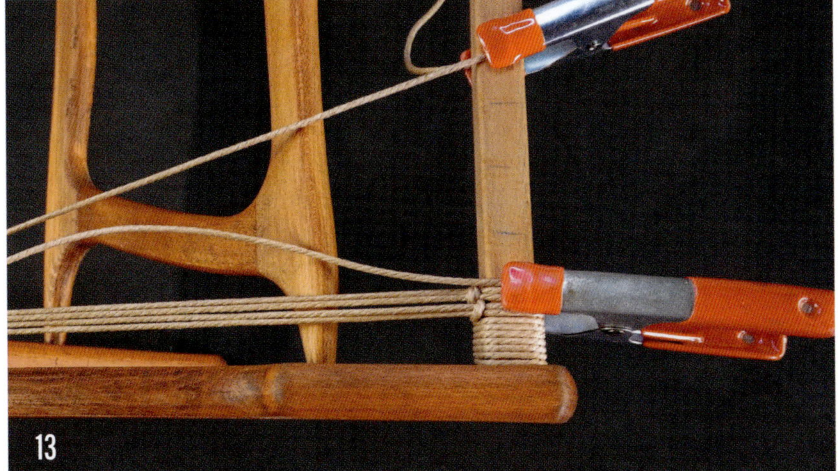
13

14 & 15

12 Tension the first strand of the pair and the bead on the back rail. Bring the strand/coil over the front rail and clamp it slightly down from the last clamped strand.

13 Tension the second part of the pair and the bead on the front rail. Clamp on the front rail.

14 Repeat steps 11-13 until you have three warp pairs (six warp strands). Compress the warp pairs, ensuring that they stay side by side—the two strands in a pairing can jump on top of each other within the bead. *It's best to angle the beads consistently to maximize compression.*

15 Keep adding rail wraps and three sets of two warp strands (Steps 3-14) until both rails are full. Don't forget to compress the material on the rails. Go slowly and be patient with yourself. It takes a while to settle into a rhythm with this pattern.

ENDING THE WARP—SEAT & BACK

16 Fully wrap the back rail, then cut the back coil, leaving ~2' as a working end. *Leave the front coil clamped and don't cut off any length.*

17 Loosen the final wraps on the back rail and tuck the end through the loosened wraps.

18 Retighten the loops and pull the working end taut. Make sure the tuck stays hidden on the inside of the rail and cut off excess material carefully.

If you are concerned about the wraps coming loose, add a tack/ staple to the tucked strand.

17

18

SKILL // JOINING WARP STRANDS

You are unlikely to run out of material while wrapping the warp strands, but it happens. You can join a new strand using a square-knot that lands on the inside of the thicker front rail.

Alternatively, you can use the rail wraps to hold the ends in place. [Refer to Skill: Splicing Weft Strands—Back, on page 149]

WEAVING THE SEAT

Due to slots in the frame, you have to weave one strand at a time instead of using a coil. Weave using a loop instead of the end of the strand to reduce kinks and make your life easier.

1

2

1 If you have material left over from the warping process at the front, thread the cord through the slot from the inside of the chair to the outside. Use a clamp on the final wraps on the front rail to keep them tensioned while you secure the transition from warp to weft. Pull the entire length of material through the slot and tension it until the front rail wraps stay snug. Then, pull the length through the handle in preparation for weaving. If you are short on material and ended your working strand on the front rail, you will need to start a new strand. [Refer to Skill: Starting a New Strand, on page 144]

2 Weave the working loop of material across the seat, moving over/under warp strand groupings. It doesn't matter whether you choose to start "over" or "under."

SKILL // WEFT TENSION

Strands should be taut, but slightly serpentine. The most important aspect is to keep the tension uniform. Pulling tighter on a few strands in a grouping will make the other strands look loose.

WEAVING THE SEAT (CONTINUED)

3 Loosely "Make a Bead—Style 1" at the left rail, then complete the first woven pair by weaving the working loop through the seat matching the over/under pattern of the previously woven strand.

4 Loosely "Make a Bead—Style 2" at the right rail.

5 Tension the pair and both beads. The slot should hold tension while you weave the next pair, but use a clamp if necessary.

6 Repeat steps 2-5 two more times until you have fully tensioned three weft pairs (six weft strands). Then compress the material on the rail.

SKILL // MAKE A BEAD

Style 1: Threading the Loop

- Bring the working loop over/around the left rail and through the slot moving from outside to inside the rail. Pull all excess material through the slot.
- Pull the working loop between the front rail and the first weft strand, over that strand and through the slot moving from inside to outside of the rail. Pull all excess material through the slot.
- Bring the working loop over the top of the left rail and through the loop you just made. Pull all excess material through the slot.

Style 2: Loop the Pair

- Same beading process used on the front rail of the warp.
- Pull the working loop over the right rail and through the slot, running from outside to inside the rail. Pull all excess material through the slot.
- Pull the working loop under the un-beaded pair, over the pair from front to back and through the slot moving from inside to outside of the rail.
- Pull all excess material through the slot.

SKILL // ENDING A STRAND

When you finish weaving the front section, or when you run out of material, you'll need to secure the end. Thread the end under the last two beads to secure. Here's how to do it:

- Loosen the last two beads on the side rail at the end of the cord. You'll have to loosen one bead on the opposite side to make this happen.

- Thread the end of the strand under the last two weft pairs between the beads and the slot. Bring the end down below the seat to tension later.
- Tension the beads and strands starting at the last anchor point. Tension the last bead by pulling the end of the cord down on the bottom of the seat.
- Trim the end of the cord carefully.

Note: It isn't necessary to add tape to the end, especially blue tape. We used it so you could see the knot easier.

7 Weave, bead and tension the next six strands while going opposite of the first six strands.

8 Continue with this alternating pattern of six strands until you run out of space in the front slot. Three sets of six strands usually fit, but every chair is different. For aesthetic reasons, it's best not to weave partial sets of six. End with a full set and spread them out to fill the slot instead.

9 End the strand securely, fix any spacing issues and tidy any unruly beads or pairs. [See Skill: Ending a Strand, at left]

WEAVING THE SEAT (CONTINUED)

10 Start a new strand to begin weaving the back section of the seat.

11 Continue to weave, bead, tension and compress on the rails while working your way toward the back of the seat. Each set of three weft pairs (six weft strands) is woven opposite to the previous set. Splice on new strands when necessary.

SKILL // COMPRESSING MATERIAL

Aim for maximum material on the rail. Angle all beads in the same direction for uniform compression. Compress on the rails periodically. [Refer to Materials, Tools & Skills Library]

SKILL // STARTING A NEW STRAND

- Create a loose pair including beads.

- Thread the end of the cord through the slot from outside to inside, under the weft pair and between the bead and side rail.

- Tension by holding the loose strand at the outside of the right slot and barely pull the front strand taut. Tighten the bead on the left side. Pull the second strand taut and tighten the bead on the right side while making sure the end of the cord (~2") runs along the top of the slot.
- Weave the next 2-3 weft pairs and beads to fully secure the end.

Note: It isn't necessary to add tape to the end, especially blue tape. We used it here so you could see the knot easier.

FINISHING THE SEAT

Most of the time, the original weaving ends at the end of the slot. We prefer to fill the extra space next to the back rail to prevent sagging and shifting of the weave. Many weavers use this trick to prolong the lifespan of the chair.

12a

12b

12c

12d

12 You can finish the weft with an ending knot at the side rail or use the following techniques to fill in the area along the curved back rail.

- Three strands in a bead **[a]**
- Create an "Over" pattern by splitting the warp grouping. **[b]**
- Create an "Under" pattern by splitting the warp grouping. Tightened, it looks like a bead. **[c, d]**

FINISHING THE SEAT (CONTINUED)

13 End with a clean knot underneath. The purpose is to end the strand elegantly and not to prevent the weave from unraveling. Any knot is acceptable.

On an "Under" pattern, send the working strand to the bottom by wrapping around one of the warp pairs. This will look like a bead on the top of the seat.

Wrap the working strand fully around itself.

Pull the working strand through the loop you just made.

14 Clip the end carefully. And celebrate a completed seat!

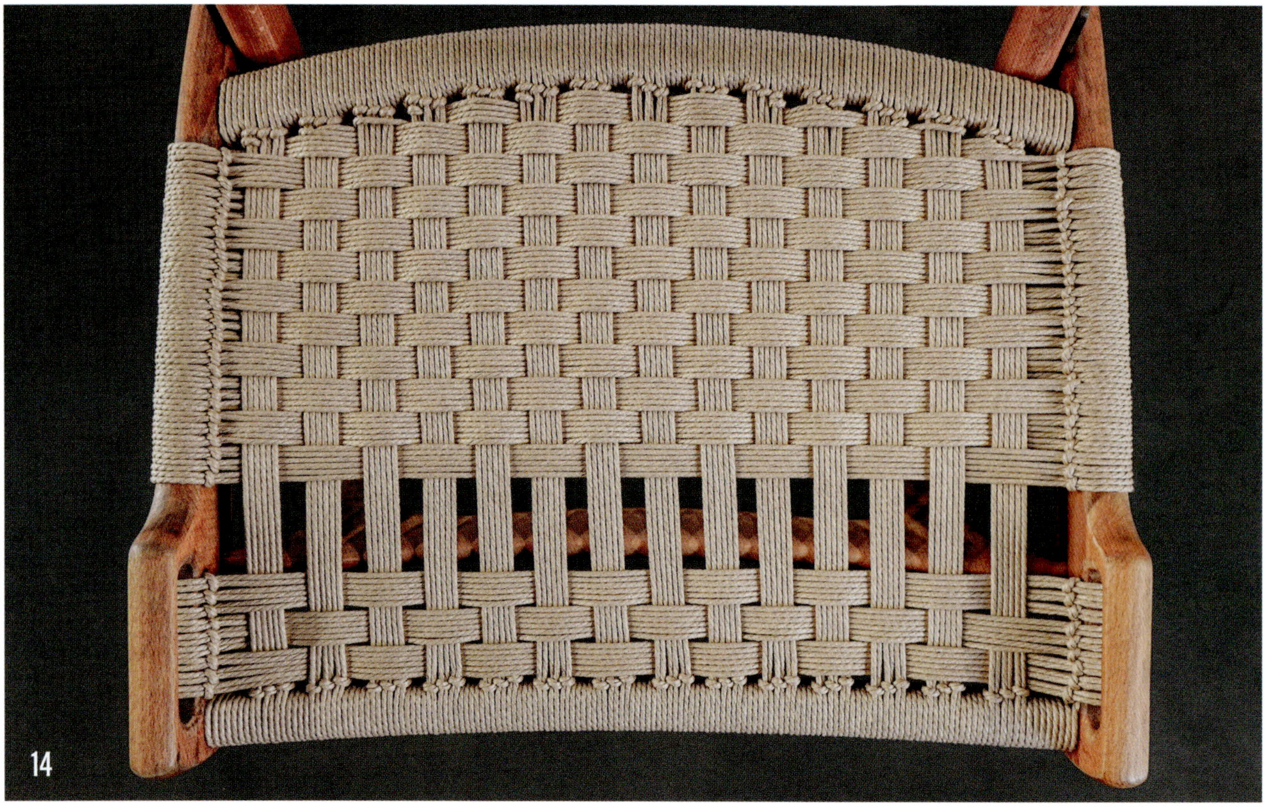

14

WEAVING THE BACK

For ergonomic purposes, we prefer to weave facing the back of the frame. The following instructions are oriented that way. Remember we are demonstrating a different pattern on the back because we see it regularly. You can also weave the back in groupings of six as you did on the seat so the seat and back are the same. This alternate pattern requires an odd number of warp groupings and weaving a double-strand. The strands will try to cross over each other, so make sure they are not crossed before tensioning. Weaving with a "working loop" and not the end of the double-strand helps prevent twists.

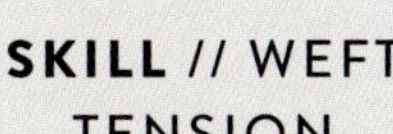

SKILL // WEFT TENSION

The wraps around the post should be tight while the woven strands should be taut, but slightly serpentine. If you pull the weft strands too tight, they won't push together and form a clean pattern. The initial double-strand is especially hard to tension properly. Try to emphasize the serpentine nature, but don't obsess over it. Use a clamp on the side posts to hold tension in the wraps or woven pair.

1 Start with ~½ lb to 1 lb of material. Uncoil it, put the two ends together and find the middle. Move 2-3 arm's lengths to one side and fold material to form a double strand, staggering the ends. You will need to splice on more material eventually and staggering the working ends spreads out the splices.

2 Tack the double-strand at the fold point to the inside of the right post.

3 Weave through pattern with the double strand going over-and-under the warp groups. Push the woven pair down close to the bottom rail, but not completely into the beading.

WEAVING THE BACK (CONTINUED)

4

5

4 Wrap around the left post completely, then weave through the pattern opposite the previous strand. You'll have four strands on the left post. Pull the wrap and weft pair taut, then push the pair down until it is barely touching the previous pair.

5 Wrap the right post and weave through the pattern going the same way as the initial strand. Pull the wrap and weft pair taut, then push the pair down until it is barely touching the previous pair.

6 Continue to weave and wrap rails, working your way up the back of the chair. Periodically compress the strands on the rail and splice in new strands when necessary.

SKILL // COMPRESS MATERIAL

Use a screwdriver like a paddle and tap it with a hammer. [Refer to Materials, Tools & Skills Library] Only compress with a hammer/screwdriver on the rails, use you hands and gently nudge the woven strands together within the panel.

SKILL // SPLICING WEFT STRANDS—BACK

By staggering the ends of the initial material "loop," you avoid ending both strands at the same time. You can add a new strand with a knot, a tack/staple or use the rail wraps to lock in the ends of both strands. If the rail wraps aren't tight enough to hold the splice secure, add a tack/staple to the joint. Compress on the rail before adding the tacks/staples.

- When you are about to wrap the post, tuck the end of the working strand under three lower wraps, creating a loop at the post. **[a]**
- Pull the loop almost taut and thread the new strand through the loop with the end pointing up the post. Clamp the end of the new strand to the post. Future wraps will hold the end of the new strand in place. **[b]**
- Pull the joined strands taut so that the junction is in the center of the inside post. **[c]**
- Continue to weave and cut the new strand after it's secured by three additional wraps.

a

b

c

Note: Wrapping tape around the end of the "working strand" (photo a) makes it easier to get under the rail wraps. The tape on the new strand (photo b) isn't necessary. We used it so you could see the splice more easily.

FINISHING THE BACK

7 You can end the weave two ways. Ideally, you can tuck the end down the post and under several wraps. This is the same method as splicing on a new strand, but without the new strand.

If you are having trouble tucking the strand down the side rail, end the weave with a knot at the top rail. Start by running one of the strands around a grouping of warp pairs and back toward the side post. Then tie a knot by forming a loop with the strand coming around the post and lacing as shown in the photo. Adjust the knot location as needed, pull the knot tight, trim the ends and tuck the knot into the pattern by the top rail. **[7a, 7b]**

(Note: It isn't necessary to add tape to the end, especially blue tape. We used tape so you could see the knot easier.)

7a back side

7b back side

MAINTENANCE

Danish cord chairs are indoor chairs! An occasional vacuuming works to remove dirt from between the cords. Danish cord is treated with wax to reduce staining, but spills can discolor it. We don't recommend spot cleaning, but according to the Carl Hansen website, it's possible to clean Danish cord with a mild, natural soap solution on an almost-dry cloth. This should be done sparingly or it will damage the cord. Avoid synthetic detergents.

DESIGN TIPS

Try different combinations of warp/weft groupings and spacing. Groups of two or four strands spaced out on the rail will significantly change the overall feel of the chair. Crunch them together for a "fabric" appearance or spread them out for a ropier/open design. Have fun with it!

Slots and the hinge mechanism are key to the aesthetic and function of this folding chair design. Make sure you have enough clearance for your material of choice to fit through the slots easily, but just barely enough room. Make sure the low-profile pin/socket hinge you choose or design can withstand the sitting forces. There is a reason this is a metal joint in the vintage designs.

Edmond Spence Yucatan Chair Courtesy of David Johnson

The weaving process presented isn't limited to Mid-Century designs or folding chairs for that matter. A Danish cord weave is incredibly comfortable, durable and applicable to most chair frames.

APPENDIX

ERGONOMICS & INJURY PREVENTION

Chronic overuse injuries happen in any trade. It won't take long to feel the effects of long term repetitive motion. Students are often surprised at how tired they are "just weaving a chair," both mentally and physically.

Aunt Linda used to say, "Make sure you charge enough to get a manicure." In reality, fingernails shred, you may get blisters or calluses, but really, YOU HAVE TO TAKE CARE OF YOUR ENTIRE BODY—your spine, your joints and muscles, your skin. We have spent thousands of dollars at the chiropractor, physical therapist, massage therapist, acupuncturist, yoga classes, and have been riddled with chronic back, neck, and shoulder issues from overworking.

The most important tool in chair weaving is your body. Check with your doctor/chiropractor/physical therapist to see if these suggestions work for your issues and your practice.

POSITIONING YOURSELF FOR SUCCESS

Pay attention to your postural habits and combat injuries before they happen.

Before, during, and after weaving. Spend some time moving your joints, gently traction your fingers, small movements in your shoulders, wrists, and elbows. Pull your belly in to support your spine. Try to keep your shoulders loosely pulled back and your chest open while you weave. Do a counterpose occasionally to compensate for all of the forward bending work. At the end of the weaving session, whether you were sitting or standing, elevate your legs to increase blood flow.

Schedule Breaks: It's easy to get lost in the process. You have to intentionally pull yourself out of the weaving groove to consider your posture, get your blood flowing, just for five minutes. Set an alarm to walk away and rest your eyes.

Working Standing Up: Stand on an anti-fatigue mat. Place the chair on a worktable so the seat is at elbow level. Worktable size depends on the weaver's height and the dimensions of the chair you are weaving. We have a low table for working on rocker backs, a thigh-high table for weaving average side chairs (usually a 17"-tall seat frame), and a waist high table for working on chair backs and seats with removable frames. If you are working too high, it puts strain on

PRO TIP:
Flipping your chair

For most types of weaving, you will have to turn the chair over repeatedly to weave through the bottom. Pretend the chair has a hinge that attaches the front legs to the work table. Step to the side and swing the back of the chair toward the floor, ending with the seat sitting flat on the work table.

Chair too far back, leaning too far forward.

Leaning into the table, lower back crunched.

Chair is close to end of table, body not leaning.

your shoulders and neck. If you are working too low, it strains your back.

Working Sitting Down: If you aren't used to standing up for 4-5 hours at a time, try using a kneeling stool and a lower table. If you sit too long in general, much less hunched over a chair, it's important to lay flat, lengthen your spine or gently twist to compensate. When you sit too long the muscles on the front body get tight. The shortened front body = an overstretched and weak back body. Ugh I know, it's hard to be human.

Move Yourself and Your Project: We are constantly catching students leaning into the table with their backs arched. If the chair has drifted away from you, pull it closer to you. Cover the worktable with a yoga mat, some foamy puzzle things, or a blanket to keep the chair from sliding around. You don't get bonus points for keeping your chair in the same position the entire time! So, make your life easier by turning it sideways, backward, upside down.

Rockers: It's hard to weave a moving target. Use a yoga mat or towel wedged under the rockers to stabilize the chair. For large rockers, there are options to access both sides of the seat that are awkward in their own ways. (1) Lay the rocker on its back and move yourself from side-to-side to access the panel. (2) Slide the rocker toward you and tip the chair backward using the rockers as a pivot point.

Extra-Large Projects: For big rockers, sofas, or deep seated chair backs, consider the amount of time you are bent awkwardly to reach around, under, and behind the chair frames. This will take a toll on your body, no matter how fit you are. Take more breaks. If you are doing this for a business, you should charge more for the physical strain (it is cumulative!) and because the piece will take up more real estate in your workshop.

BASIC SKILLS TO COMBAT FATIGUE

Sore Spine/Neck: Stabbing, burning, tingling in your neck or spine are signs that you should seek medical attention. Many issues in the spine result from it being out of alignment or from opposing muscles not doing their work. Pulling in your belly to support your spine is one of the simplest things you can do. Keeping your head high and back, shoulders down and shoulder blades pulling together can help mitigate neck issues.

Tired Legs: Squish your toes, rotate the ankles, bend and flex the knees. Do some gentle squats (with your belly pulled in). Pat down your legs to increase circulation. Try standing with one leg propped on a bucket and then switch sides regularly. Lay flat with your legs raised to increase circulation at the end of the day. Wear compression socks.

ERGONOMICS & INJURY PREVENTION (CONTINUED)

Counterpose for forward leaning while working.

Sore Hands/Arms: Some weavers quit because of arthritis and some have started weaving to help their arthritis. Warm wax dips are excellent for achy hands. Salves and creams (CBD, Arnica, Rx) are great to use when you are done for the day. Arnica and turmeric can be taken internally as an anti-inflammatory (check with your doctor).

Should you wear gloves when weaving? So much of chair weaving is tactile and even the tight, sticky gardening gloves get in the way. The exception to this rule would be for slab rattan (slices), Danish cord or paper rush (blisters).

MATERIAL SPECIFIC ISSUES

Rush: This is the most physically demanding type of weaving. New weavers may get blisters on their pointer fingers from pulling tension. Keep some tape handy if you are a newbie. Eventually your dominant shoulder and that side of your neck will experience fatigue. Many chair weavers quit rush weaving due to the toll it has taken on their elbows and shoulders. You have to turn the chair over regularly to adjust the bottom.

Splint and Binder Cane: Splint weaving is mostly hard on the hands as you pull the reed through warp strands. This chews your cuticles and dries out your hands. Binder cane is more likely to cut your hands so pay attention. USE YOUR TOOLS! You have to turn the chair over every single row to weave the bottom.

Shaker Tape: This is our favorite type of weaving. It's soft and quick. But there is a lot of pulling! And you have to turn your chair over every row.

Danish Cord: Generally, these are quick victories, unless you have split rails/slots where you have to pull the entire length of coil through over and over ... that's a ton of pulling. You may want to tape your fingers to avoid blisters. When weaving the rush pattern, plan to wear gloves. On the more common, single-panel design, you'll still have to flip the chair over occasionally to make sure the cord didn't get twisted or snagged on the nailhead.

Rotate arms like turning a door knob.

PATTERN MAPPING & EXAMPLE PATTERNS

Most alternative warp/weft patterns are a combination of twill and checkerboard. When exploring more complex patterns, here are some helpful tips.

- Determine the size of your pattern map by measuring the length of the rails and dividing that by the width of your material. (A 16" rail and ⅝" material results in 25 or 26 strands on that rail.) Once the warp strands are established, verify that your strand count is correct.
- Add the "posts" to your map to help you stay oriented.
- Does your pattern have a center? An odd number of strands on the front rail is ideal for symmetry, but not 100% necessary.
- Create your own pattern by outlining your dimensions on graph paper. Or you can use those dimensions and overlay them on an existing pattern map. Each block represents a strand of material.
- Try rotating an existing pattern 90°. You might like that pattern better.
- Materials matter when choosing or creating a pattern: You don't want the weaving to be loose or the weaving so tight that it destroys your material ... and your hands. Weaving over/under one strand with anything other than Shaker tape or some other woven fabric strap is impossible without seriously compromising the material. Here are some general guidelines. Note that narrower material allows for more intricate patterns.
- Shaker Tape - ⅝" width over/under 1-4 strands; 1" width over/under 1-3 strands
- Splint Reed - ⅜" width over/under 3-6 strands; ½" width over/under 2-5 strands; ⅝" width over/under 2-4 strands

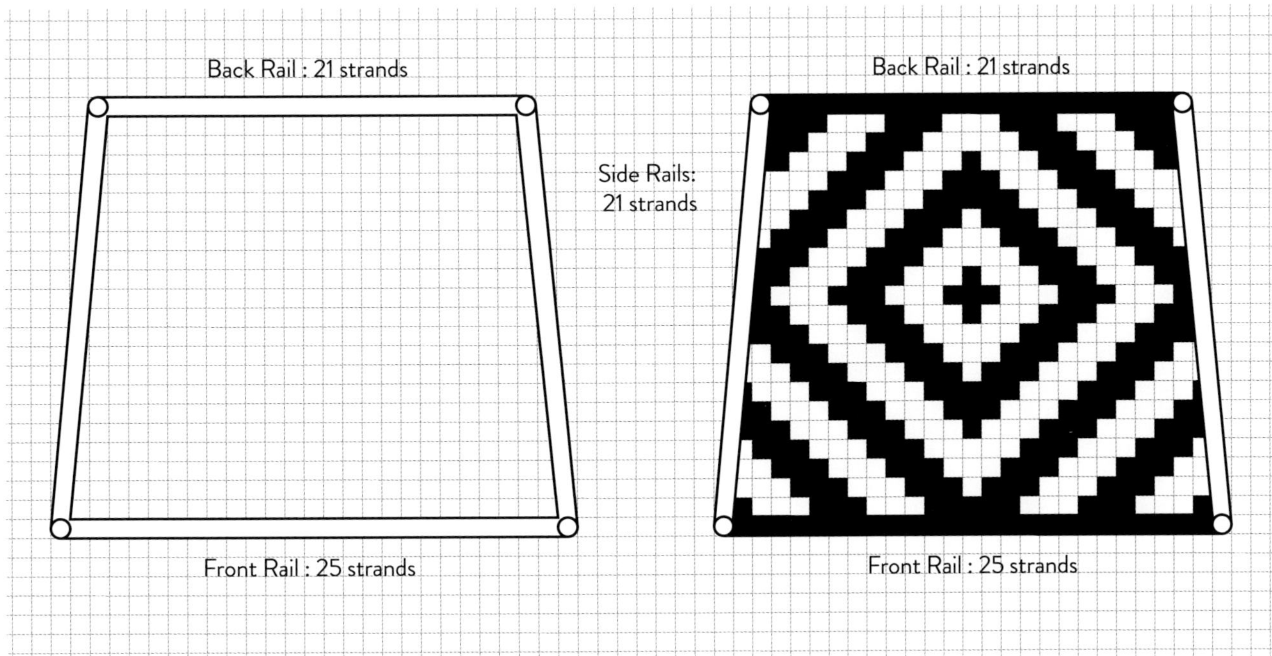

PATTERN MAPPING & EXAMPLE PATTERNS (CONTINUED)

Shaker Tape, Splint Reed, Binder Cane

Shaker Tape

Shaker Tape, Splint Reed, Binder Cane

Shaker Tape

Shaker Tape, Splint Reed, Binder Cane

Shaker Tape

Shaker Tape

Shaker Tape

FIND YOUR TRIBE!

Falling down a rabbit hole of weaving is more fun with company. Get inspired, get advice, get out there and spread the love of chairs. Make friends with furniture restorers, designers, fiber weavers, etc. The following examples are just the tip of the iceberg. Explore craft in your community. Part of the fun is discovering things on your own ... or do they discover you?

FIND & FOLLOW US:

www.instagram.com/silverriverchairs

www.facebook.com/silverrivercenterforchaircaning

@silverriverchairs on youtube.com

Search: #chairnerd #chairsofinstagram #cannage #chaircaning #wienergeflecht #canespotting #seatweaving

JOIN AN ORGANIZATION:

The Seatweavers' Guild, Inc. *seatweaversguild.org*

The Furniture Society *furnsoc.org*

The Southern Highland Craft Guild *southernhighlandguild.org*

The American Craft Council *craftcouncil.org*

Local, regional and national basketry, fiber, or furniture/woodworking organizations

Heritage Crafts, U.K. *https://heritagecrafts.org.uk*

PUT YOURSELF OUT THERE:

Weaving and Teaching Directories

www.wickerwoman.com/furniture-repair-directory

www.seatweaversguild.org/business-member-links

www.peerlessrattan.com/locate-a-caner

IN-PERSON INSTRUCTION:

Silver River Center for Chair Caning: Asheville, N.C.— Group and individual in-person classes, covering 5 basic styles of weaving and customized tutorials.

Arrowmont School of Arts and Crafts: Gatlinburg, Tenn. (most excellent corn shuck chair collection)

John C Campbell Folk School: Brasstown, N.C. (many chair seating classes and great chairs on campus)

Sue Muldoon teaches chair weaving and basketry all over the Northeast, in person and online. *reduxforyou.com*

Rachael South teaches chair weaving in England & Denis Guerin teaches chair weaving in France.

Many craft schools teach the occasional weaving class or chairmaking class with woven seating including: Haywood Community College Professional Craft program, North Bennet Street School, Penland School of Craft, Sawtooth School for Visual Art, Center for Furniture Craftsmanship, Haystack Mountain School of Craft, Port Townsend School of Woodworking, Marc Adams School of Woodworking, North House Folk School, The Woodworking School at Pinecroft, A Workshop of Our Own. Find more at *craftschools.us*

Many classes are taught at continuing education centers, craft and antique fairs, and at woodworking and weaving conferences.

ONLINE INSTRUCTION:

@silverriverchairs YouTube Channel

@peerlessrattansuppliesllc7113 YouTube Channel

Peerless Rattan: Free Online Videos
www.peerlessrattan.com/instructions

Wicker Woman: Information and Instructions
www.wickerwoman.com

Basket Maker's Supply: Free Online Videos
www.basketmakerssupply.com

BE A PART OF A GROUP ON SOCIAL MEDIA

Cane and Wicker Restoration is a worldwide public Facebook group—Post their projects, questions, and generally geek on chairs.

The SeatWeavers' Guild—private and public group pages

Facebook Basket Weavers; Basketry, gourd weaving, and more! group by The Country Seat

Women of Woodworking

Antiques, Basketry, Mid-Century, Arts and Crafts and other specialty groups, there are so many

EXPLORE THE WORLD OF CHAIRS

Go to museums, exhibits, historic homes, or living history sites. Some of our favorites that we have visited or desperately want to visit:

In Asheville, N.C.: Village Antiques, The Folk Art Center, Grovewood Gallery, Brian Boggs Chairmakers

Pleasant Hill Shaker Village, Harrodsburg, Ky., and all over Berea, Ky.

The Miller House, Columbus, Ind.

The Island Farm, Manteo, N.C.

Yale University Decorative Arts Gallery,
New Haven, Conn.

The Art of Seating: 200 Years of American Design (travels the country)

In Europe: Victoria and Albert Museum, London; Vitra Design Museum, Weil am Rhein, Germany; Danish Design Museum, Copenhagen, Denmark; Museum of Applied Arts, Vienna

REFERENCE BOOKS

BOOKS ON CHAIR SEAT WEAVING & RATTAN

with a note from Brian Crossley, MBE, who contributed a significant portion of the list. I was pleased to find most of them already in our Chair Library and added a few to the list.

"An important aspect to bear in mind is that no book contains all the unique tips and details of the crafts when using woven seating materials, which would normally only be conveyed during teaching. It is strongly suggested that if the reader does not have access to an expert Teacher, that they refer to a selection of books on the craft to access these details. Many of the books listed below are now out of print but they can be borrowed from your local Library to access information unique to each book."
—Brian Crossley, Chester U.K.

Chair Seating—Techniques in Cane, Rush, Willow and Cords, by Kay Johnson, Olivia Elton Barratt and Mary Butcher. ISBN 0-85219-736-5. Hardback. 192 pages. First edition published by Dryad Press Ltd in 1988, reprinted 1990. Now out of print, but copies of a reprint in a spiral bound paperback format are available from Mary Butcher in the U.K. or from Silver River Chairs in the U.S.

Seat Weaving, by Ricky Holdstock. ISBN 0-946819-46-7. Paperback. 151 pages. First edition published by Guild of Master Craftsmen 1989. Reprinted in a different extended Paperback format by Guild of Master Craftsmen ISBN 0-946819-16-5 undated, 144 pages.

Cane and Rush Seating by Margery Brown ISBN 0-7134-4620 X . Paperback. 96 pages. First published 1976 by BT Batsford Ltd. Reprinted 1977, 1984, 1989.

Cane and Rush Seating by David and Freda Broan ISBN 0-900873-41-8. Paperback 120 pages. Published 1981 by Whistable Litho Ltd.

Chair Seat Weaving by George Sterns ISBN 0-934026-56-4. Paperback 159 pages. Published 1990 by Interweave Press, Colorado.

How to Make Your Own Cane Furniture by Max and Charlotte Alth ISBN 0-85442 021 5. Hardback 216 pages. First published in 1979 in the U.S.

Cane, Rush and Willow by Hilary Burns ISBN 1-55209-267-7. Paperback 144 pages. Published 1998 by Quintet Publishing Ltd.

Making Chair Seats from Cane, Rush and other Natural Materials by Ruth B. Comstock. ISBN 0-486-25693-6. Paperback 44 pages. First published in Canada in 1988.

The Caner's Handbook by Bruce W Miller and Jim Widess. ISBN 0-00-411772-7. 139 pages. First published in U.S. in 1983. Updated and revised version published 2024: ISBN 978-0-7643-6763-2.

The Complete Guide to Chair Caning by Jim Widess. ISBN 1-57990-613-3. Hardback 127 pages. Published 2005 by Lark Books.

Canework by Charles Crampton Published by Dryad Press 1953.

Cannez Rempaillez vos Chaises by Denis Guérin. ISBN 2-04 721887-X Hardback. 95 pages. Published 2001 by Dessain et Tolra.

American Seating Furniture 1630–1730 by Benno M. Forman ISBN 0-393-02516-0 Hardback. 397 pages. Published 1988 by W.W. Norton & Company Ltd. The collection of American furniture in the Winterthur Museum, Del. Appendix contains a translation of the earliest known detailed description (and diagrams) of the "six-way caning pattern" used in most Chair Caning. The original is in Volume 2 of "Description des arts et métiers" (1745-1761) by André Jacob Roubo.

The Nature and Culture of Rattan. Reflections on Vanishing Life in the Forests of Southeast Asia by Stephen F Siebert. ISBN 978-0-8248-3536-1. Hardback. 145 pages. Published 2012 by University of Hawai'i Press.

Backwoods Chairmakers—In Search of the Appalachian Ladderback Chairmaker by Andrew D. Glenn. ISBN 978-1-954697-17-1. 2023 Lost Art Press.

Just One Good Chair Christian Holmsted Olesen Danish Design Museum (book doesn't have usual copyright info).

Now I Sit Me Down, From Klismos to Plastic Chair: A Natural History. By Witold Rybczynski. ISBN 978-0-374-22321-2. 2016. Farrar, Straus and Giroux.

Traditionell Rottingflätning by Pernilla Blixt. ISBN 978-91-527-4958-6. In Swedish but extremely helpful instructions, interesting historical images. 140 pages on hand-woven chair caning. 2022.

Benches, Stools, and Chairs—A Guide to Ergonomic Woven Seating by Walter Turpening and Deborah Held. ISBN 978-0-8117-7050-7. 2022 Stackpole Books.

Chair Caning & Seat Weaving Handbook Illustrated Directions for Cane, Rush, and Tape Seats by Editors of Skills Institute Press. ISBN 978-1-56523-556-4. 2012 Fox Chapel Publishing.

The Art of Seating 200 Years of American Design by Brian J. Lang. ISBN 978-1-913875-21-3. 2022. The Thomas H. and Diane DeMell Jacobsen Ph.D Foundation in association with The Mint Museum, Charlotte N.C.

The Antique Hunter's Guide. American Furniture: Tables, chairs, sofas, & beds. By Marvin D Schwartz. ISBN 1-57912-108-X. 2000 Chanticleer Press Inc.

Pleasant Hill Shaker Furniture by Kerry Pierce. ISBN 978-1-55870-795-5. 2007.

Ideas for the Experienced Caner #1 and #2 by John and Lillian Peterka, 1975 & 1977. Self-published pamphlets.

CHAIR SEAT WEAVING AS A BUSINESS: PRICING CONSIDERATIONS & BUSINESS PRACTICES

- Start pricing at your confidence level and incrementally increase as your skills improve.
- Decide how much work you put into the projects and if you are doing this as sole income or hobby.
- Be honest about your skill level/experience and guarantee your work.
- An average chair measures (across the widest measurement only) are commonly 17" for a seat, except Mid-century Danish Cord Chairs which are almost always around 18".
- Time to complete the project includes removal of old material, prepping of chair frame, potential structural work, weaving, finishing/sealing the seat, potential reconstruction of decorative elements.

PAPER FIBER RUSH

Time to complete a project: 1-3 days/panel. Chairs with slots and tiny cords priced higher.

Advanced: Windsor/Hitchcock chairs may need to be deconstructed and reconstructed before and after the weaving process may require coordination with a furniture refinisher. Detachable frames can be trickier.

PRE-TWISTED NATURAL RUSH

Time to complete the project: 1-3 days/panel. Material is more expensive and there is more waste. Advanced methods are similar to paper rush.

BASIC SPLINT WEAVE (≥ ½")

Time to complete the project: 1-4 days/panel. Advanced patterns and large rockers, chairs with curved backs, and Dyed Reed, price slightly higher.

SPLINT/BINDER CANE (< ½" WIDE)

Time to complete the project: 2-5 days/panel ... tedious work ¼" at a time, especially on large rockers or backs with slots.

AUTHENTIC HICKORY BARK

Time to complete the project: 5-7 days including shaving of bark, weaving, allowing bark to dry, oiling, and waiting for oil to absorb, removing excess. Materials are expensive and hard to come by. Does not include the week of work it takes to harvest the bark.

SHAKER TAPE (1" WIDE—UP TO TWO COLORS)

Time to complete the project: 2-3 hours/panel

SHAKER TAPE (⅝" WIDE—UP TO TWO COLORS)

Time to complete the project: 3-5 hours/panel

If you play with multiple colors on either size, you have to sew on splices. This will only take about an hour more. If your chair

BASIC DANISH CORD

Time to complete the project: four hours. If more than a few new nails are needed add the cost of new nails. If converting from upholstery or anything involving staples add a couple of hours to the time just to remove all the staples. Split rail Danish cord weaving requires a lot of shoulder work pulling material around the split rails and increases time by about two hours. Yugoslavian folding chairs and Wegner chairs with seat and back woven take 8-10 hours to complete.

RE-GLUE OF RAILS

Time to complete and wait for glue to dry: 1 day—occasionally you can weave with the chair strapped and don't have to wait.

CLEANING FEE FOR ESPECIALLY DIRTY/MOLDY CHAIRS

This can take a day from start to finish including drying. Customers can easily do this on their own. Charge appropriately.

TUNG OIL (OUTDOORS) OR HOWARD FEED-N-WAX (INDOORS)

*Not for shiny lacquered finishes. Generally takes an hour for Feed-N-Wax to absorb. Tung oil may take about a day. Both process should include a final wipe down of excess oils. When in doubt, consult a furniture restoration professional.

PICK-UP & DELIVERY

Base fees on mileage and consider the time you spend going to and from the customers home.

COORDINATING WITH FURNITURE REFINISHERS

Necessary, but does take time and coordination of schedules. Offer this for no charge while you are developing a relationship. This gives you an opportunity to see their work and their work ethic. You both can determine if there will be a shared fee. They could be making money off of your work. You should cover your costs based on the time it takes to pick up and drop off at their shop. After you are established, just give the customer the furniture refinisher›s card.

Do **not** try staining on a customer's chair. Practice before you offer this service. Practice on scrap or on a hidden area before committing. Or just work with reliable refinishers. We have gotten burned trusting that someone knew what they were doing. We have had to pay refinishers to fix our mistakes when we tried to match a new chair with the rest of the set. It's almost impossible to match a newly woven chair with the rest of the set that has years of use/patina.

THE CURSE OF THE BARGAIN & THE HARD DEADLINE

- It is important to overestimate your deadline so you don't feel pressure. Always ask the client if they need the chair by a certain date and "do your best to accommodate."
- People will ask for a discount if they give you all the chairs at once. This is basically asking you to do more work for less money. Doing a set of rush chairs is physically demanding. Consider doing part of the set, taking a break, then doing the rest of the set later.
- Every single time we have given a hard deadline or a bargain, we have regretted it. Consider your life and your family, rest and fun outside of chairs, and then consider all of the crazy stuff that can happen not limited to catching a cold, having car repairs, global pandemics. It's better to overestimate the cost and surprise them by going down on your cost than it is to underestimate the work and hate the project since you're barely getting paid.

IT'S OK TO SAY NO

- If you are uncomfortable with the chair.
- If you get an odd feeling about the client.
- If you initially said yes to the chair and then have challenges, personal or professional.
- If you don't like that type of work (rush weaving most often!).
- If you are overwhelmed with your waitlist.

DOCUMENT YOUR CHAIRS

- Note condition of chairs while customer is present.
- Take photos of chairs before you remove the seat.
- Take close-ups of damage to the chair so you aren't held accountable.
- Take notes of the weaving process so you can recall time spent, issues, communication, etc.
- Take process photos to show the client or potential clients.
- Take "after" photos for your portfolio—before and after photos side-by-side are often dramatic!

CONSIDER

- Pick up and delivery take time and expense for gas—they can drop off for a lot less hassle to you if you're comfortable with that.
- Sales tax, Self-Employment Tax, Overhead costs, etc.
- Credit card fees can add up over time (depending on your workflow, thousands/year).

IS THE CHAIR WORTH THE RESTORATION COST?

If you want to use the chair, it's worth the investment. The frame has proven its longevity. Compared to a cell phone, which you spend hundreds to thousands on every few years, it's a better return on investment (20-50 years).

"Should I restore it if I'm going to sell it?" No, typically, the restoration fee exceeds the sellable value. Pass the cost along to the buyer.

POSTSCRIPT:

Aunt Linda's Rules of Chair Caning Business (Linda and I have broken all of these rules to our detriment)

- We don't do wicker.
- We don't stain cane.
- Take the check directly to the bank.

Postscript to the postscript: Please try wicker; you may like it. It really is an endangered craft. There are historically significant pieces out there that need restoring.

SUPPLIERS

Easy Online Links—*SilverRiverChairs.com/resources*

The following list is not all-inclusive (U.S. businesses only) and we apologize for anyone that we left out. Let us know and we'll include you on our website and, chair-gods willing, the next edition of this instructional manual. If you don't already know, most of these companies are small, family-run operations. Be kind to them and your materials are more likely to behave.

Basket Maker's Supply: Taylorsville, Ky.
basketmakerssupply.com
info@basketmakerssupply.com
(800) 447-7008

Breuer Chair Company: Farmingdale, N.Y.
breuerchaircompany.com
(855) 789-0501
[Cesca Chair—Replacement Parts]

Caning Shop: Berkeley, Calif.
caning.com
jim@caning.com
(800) 544-3373

Country Seat: Kempton, Pa.
countryseat.com
orders@countryseat.com
(610) 756-6124

Cane & Basket Supply: Los Angeles
caneandbasket.com
info@caneandbasket.com
(800) 468-3966

Earth Guild: Asheville, N.C.
earthguild.com
contact@earthguild.com
(800) 327-8448

Frank's Cane and Rush Supply: Huntington Beach, Calif.
franksupply.com
orders@frcrs.com
(714) 847-0707

Gina's Baskets: Rothbury, Mich.
ginasbaskets.com
gina@ginasbaskets.com
(231) 215-6575
[Custom Dyed Reed]

HH Perkins: North Haven, Conn.
hhperkins.com
info@hhperkins.com
(800) 462-6660

Peerless Rattan: Plainwell, Mich.
peerlessrattan.com
sales@peerlessrattan.com
(269) 993-0829

Royalwood, Ltd: Mansfield, Ohio
royalwoodltd.com
orders@royalwoodltd.com
(800) 526-1630
[Wholesale & Retail]

Shaker Workshops: N.H.
shakerworkshops.com
service@shakerworkshops.com
(800) 840-9121
[Shaker tape, furniture, more]

Silver River Center for Chair Caning: Asheville, N.C.
silverriverchairs.com
silverriverchairs@gmail.com
(828) 707-4553 [Tools & Chair Nerd Merchandise]

Suzanne Moore's N.C. Basket Works: Vass, N.C.
ncbasketworks.com
sales@ncbasketworks.com
(800) 338-4972

Troutman Chair Company: Troutman, N.C.
kennedyrockers.com
(877) 886-0992
[Kennedy Rocker Replacement Seat & Back]

V.I. Reed & Cane: Omaha, Neb.
seatweaving.org
vireedandcane@gmail.com

INSPIRATION GALLERY

Photo by Anthony Harden

Djemebe-stitched Leather and Rawhide Rocker by Brandy Clements and Barbara Walker.

Log Cabin Weave with Custom-Gradient Flat-braided Cord by Brandy Clements.

Photo by Robert Grand.

Chair by Zak Foster.

Woven Belt Chairs by Sue Muldoon.

Multi-color Polypropylene Cord Stool by Sue Muldoon.

Plaid Shaker Tape Stool by David Klingler.

INSPIRATION GALLERY (CONTINUED)

CONTEMPORARY CHAIRMAKERS

“Anyone for Tennis?” by Rebecca Juliette-Deux

Metal Sculpture—Splint Two-Slat Sidechairs by Sophie Glen.

Metal Sculpture—Rush Corner Chair by Sophie Glen.

Metal Sculpture—Rush Ladderback by Sophie Glen.

“Both Sides Now” by Rebecca Juliette-Deux

CONTEMPORARY CHAIRMAKERS

Danish Cord Rush by Charlie Ryland.

Danish Cord Rush by Robel Awake.

Danish Cord Rush by Robel Awake.

INSPIRATION GALLERY (CONTINUED)

CONTEMPORARY WOVEN FURNITURE

Kate Casey of Peg Woodworking, Brooklyn, N.Y.

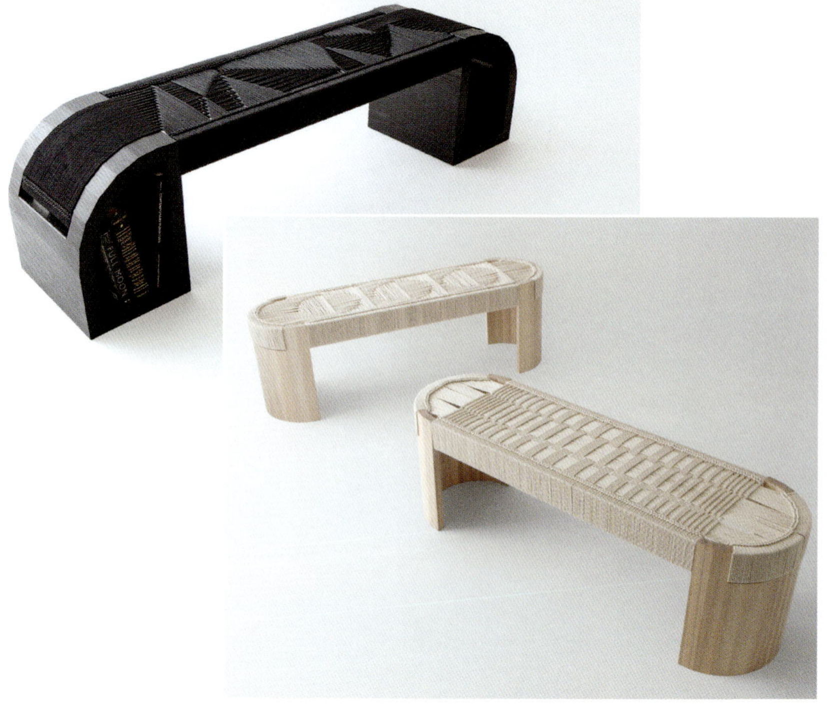

THE FAIR ISLE CHAIR

On the Heritage Craft Association's Red List of Endangered Craft. This straw-back chair is being revived by Eve Eunson, Fair Isle, Shetland, Scotland.

ACKNOWLEDGMENTS

Love to Brandy's chair weaving family: Aunt Linda, Bill, Hobert and Ida Clements, Dick Allen. My dad (also Hobert Clements) put me on a path, the outcome of which is tbd, but has been a wild ride. Our chair weaving shop/school/museum is a tribute to his memory. My sister Christy gives us invaluable legal advice ... go write one of the books in your head. Mom and Frank, our cheerleaders, thank you for your confidence and financial support during the writing of the book and covid times. This book wouldn't exist without you. And to Dave, my kitten, who puts up with my back going out, my crazy schemes and insatiable travel bug. Your brain works in ways mine just doesn't and the business is better for it. Rosie, our director of customer relations and photography assistant, never chewed a chair leg and is always excited for a new day. Jack Dog was my original travel buddy—we started the first chair shop because we didn't want to go to work without him.

To Dave's grandfather, Harry, who gave full access to his woodworking tools ... as long as I didn't get hurt. To my parents, Richard and Nancy, who provided a workshop for me to hide away in when I needed it most. Your support allowed me to find a new path. Love you guys! To Brandy, my teacher, partner and co-conspirator in our worldwide, weaving adventure. Thank you for your patience and understanding when I lost myself down my own rabbit holes, worked myself to exhaustion, and spent WAY too much time organizing instead of actually doing. My life is infinitely more interesting because I share it with you.

To David Johnson of Sidecar Furniture (and Bowie, best shop dog on the West Coast) our Instagram bestie and eventual Chair Nerd podcast co-host, thanks for working on this while you had covid. To Bob Haase, for pushing us out of the nest, providing the woodworking safety net, and for taking us kayaking. Joe McCarson and Tim McCall for providing structural work services and general business commiserations over the years. To Leanne Apfelbeck, our chiropractor, who saves us when we are broken and keeps us upright.

Our hosts at Arrowmont, Campbell Folk School, The Island Farm, and other museums, and podcasts hosts have been kind enough to invite us to share our love of chairs. Adam at Shaker Workshops gave us a tour and epicly warm Tappan Chairs hats. Rick and Lucy Daley provided the missing link: the Yugoslavian Folding Chair—from the estate of Betty and Richard Daley. Scott Woody of Woody's Chair Shop donated the rush chair. David Douyard contributed the bark images and was responsible for a fantastic afternoon sitting in handmade Windsor chairs, drinking craft beers and talking shop. Cathryn Peters contributed information, advice, and images for cattail rush. Zack Foster, Robert Garland, Denis Guerin, David Johnson, Eve Eunson and Becca Van K contributed inspiring chair images. Pleasant Hill Shaker Village contributed historical images. Andy Glenn contributed bark advice, harvesting images, and book commiseration—buy his Backwoods Chairmakers book! Caleb James and David Johnson helped us fine tune Danish weaving advice: both teach classes! Mitch and Deb Palminteri of Friend of Furniture took on the burden of our restoration waitlist so we could focus, and made our sad splint chair frame happy. Barbara and Mike Walker let us invade their home with lighting equipment and 50 chairs. Chad and Liz Conaty shared their cozy office space when writing was too difficult at the shop. James and Sunny Carr allowed us to shoot glamor shots of chairs at their beautiful home. Grovewood Gallery welcomes us with wide arms and smiling faces and allowed us to shoot some glamor shots at Grovewood Village.

To all our friends who make life in Asheville so special. Thank you for breaking bread with us, sharing drinks with us and encouraging us along the way. It is 100% generic to say and 100% true ... there are too many people that helped, inspired and influenced this project to thank properly.

Thanks to the Blue Hills Press team for their patience and taking a chance on us. Thanks for making the book look amazing. And, of course, to the readers, weavers, learners and browsers ... thanks for purchasing this book! It has been a Brave and Dandy adventure for us and we hope for all of you too!

INDEX

INDEX (CONTINUED)

T

W

Y